FIRESIDE

Marie Osmond's Guide to Beauty,

Health, and Style

by MARIE OSMOND
with Julie Davis

A Fireside Book
Published by
Simon and Schuster
New York

Designed by Elizabeth Woll
Manufactured in the United States of America

1   2   3   4   5   6   7   8   9   10
1   2   3   4   5   6   7   8   9   10   *Pbk.*

Library of Congress Cataloging in Publication Data

Osmond, Marie, date.
  Marie Osmond's Guide to beauty, health, and style.

  1. Beauty, Personal.   2. Young women—Health and
hygiene.   3. Fashion.   4. Young women—Conduct of
life.   I. Davis, Julie, joint author.   II. Title.
III. Title: Guide to beauty, health, and style.
RA778.75   646.7'2   79-22504
ISBN 0-671-24686-0
ISBN 0-671-25350-6 Pbk.

Acknowledgments

I WISH TO express a special "thank you" to those beautifully talented people, whose artistic skills together make the total look of glamor: Ret Turner, Gail Rowell, Bob Ryan, Harry Langdon, Stan McBean, Suga, Way Bandy, Richard Avedon, Bjorn, Maurice Andre, Bob Mackie, Marlow J. Lee, Merrett Smith, and especially to my family, whose patience, understanding, and counsel have given me confidence and self-worth. Without them, there would have been no Marie Osmond. And to Julie Davis. What a friend . . . a cherished, wonderful friend whose writing talent stands among the greats!

Marie Osmond

I WOULD LIKE to pay tribute to Dr. Stuart Froum, whose commitment to preventative dentistry teaches us one of the most important beauty lessons we can learn, one that offers the greatest beauty reward: a perfect smile.

Julie Davis

WE WOULD LIKE to acknowledge our beautiful young editor, Ann-Marie Miller, who first conceived of the idea for this book and whose dedicated editorial guidance helped bring it to fruition.

Marie and Julie

To our mothers,
Olive and Rochelle,
who taught us that true beauty
starts from within

Contents

PHOTOCRAFT

1.
From Me to You

I LOVE PERFORMING for many reasons but mostly because of all the girls I get to meet. It's like having hundreds of friends—except that you often know more about me than I do about you. One thing I'm sure of is that we have a lot in common. We all want to learn about and experience those special moments that make being a girl so special. Makeup, fashion, dating—it seems as though we can never discover them soon enough!

Being in the public eye has given me a great advantage: I can share with you all the secrets I've learned during my teens, those exceptionally exciting and at times difficult years. Television and magazines tell you something about me, but there's much more I think you'd like to know. I'm grateful for this chance to talk to you because I know that what I do, how I dress and wear my hair influence a lot of my fans—maybe you! Writing a book is, for me, an opportunity to tell you what I've learned and to answer those questions I'm most frequently asked. For you, it's a way to explore all the fun things we've all looked forward to since we were little. And for *us*, you and me, it's time to get a little better acquainted.

Girls often tell me that I'm lucky because I have a career, or because I'm thin, or know how to apply makeup. But it's not really a question of being lucky at all. In fact, not so long ago I had a chunky figure, and because of it I felt inferior; I was shy and self-conscious. I couldn't even dream about performing with my brothers; I was afraid of embarrassing them. When I really came to grips with myself, I realized that my problems were my own fault, and if I really wanted to, I could work to solve them.

What finally got me started was hearing that my younger brother Jimmy had earned a gold record. I wanted to contribute to my family, too. That meant taking positive action, something every girl can do.

Sometimes we feel that our problems are hopeless, and we

wonder why all the other girls we know seem so perfect. Well, the situation is really never that unbalanced. Even those enviable friends of ours could use a little extra help (or have taken the same steps I will describe on the following pages!). I've seen my friends change their personalities in only two hours, just by learning to use cosmetics. Sure, it's going to be dull at first, while you're practicing the same makeup routine, but once you know the basics, you can start experimenting as I do. (Some days, I spend only ten minutes applying my makeup, while on others, I can take as long as two hours!)

But being pretty on the outside is only part of a girl's beauty. A woman who is really beautiful has more than physical appeal. She has class—a certain style and grace all her own, a way of walking and talking that tells the world she's a very special person. Some people say it means having a lot of money. That's not true. When a girl walks into a room and is noticed because of the way she carries herself, it doesn't matter if she has only two pennies in her purse. She has a sense of confidence that comes from caring about herself and knowing that she looks and feels the best she can. We are all blessed, though in different ways. All we have to do is learn to make the most of our individual assets.

The kind of girl you want to be depends on your attitude. You really have to want to be talented or thin or self-confident—or all three, if you're like me! It's important while working on the inner you to make yourself interesting by discovering the world around you: going to school and enjoying it, reading about world situations and listening as other people speak. The result is knowing how to talk to anyone about practically anything rather than being able to talk only about yourself.

Poise is a quality you don't hear much about today, but it's as necessary as ever. Poise is feeling comfortable in every situation. It's knowing the right way to look and act—knowing not only what to say, but how to say it. Girls with poise aren't afraid of trying something new because it might mess their hair or wrinkle their skirt. It's learning to be at ease with yourself.

Traveling, working with fashion designers, makeup artists and hair stylists, performing and living with eight brothers, and having two of the most wonderful parents in the world have given me a special education. But even more special is that I can share it all with you. I can't think of anything more fun than that!

Beauty and Health:
A Winning Combination

WHEN I meet girls who ask me to make them look prettier, I always tell them to start by taking better care of themselves—their nails, their hair, their skin, even their eyelashes!

There are really two kinds of care: beauty care and health care. Beauty care improves the outer you with cosmetics, lotions, and potions. But the outer you is a direct reflection of the inner you and the care you take to see to it that you have a healthy body. To be pretty on the outside, you really have to be pretty on the inside.

All it takes is simple things, such as washing your face before going to sleep (so that pimples don't have a chance to form in clogged pores), eating the right foods that promote a clear complexion and shiny hair, brushing your teeth after meals, etc. That kind of early care, before you even begin to think of makeup and painting your nails, is the best head start to becoming a pretty girl . . . and a prettier woman.

Let me show you what I mean.

2.
The Beauty Part: Complexion Care

IF YOU'RE LIKE me, you'd rather read about makeup than skin care. Makeup is fun; skin care sounds like a boring routine. But I wish that I could tell every girl just how important caring for your complexion is. You may think of a makeup product as being the foundation for your skin, but your complexion is the real foundation for makeup. You can put all the cosmetics in the world on your face, but without a clear, healthy complexion, they won't make much difference.

Taking the right steps in complexion care begins before you even think of wearing makeup. While you're young, cleansing with a mild glycerine soap is probably enough. But when your body starts to mature, it's as though an alarm goes off. Now is the time to look closely at your complexion and read all the signals it's sending you.

There are four different types of complexions, and each one has a care plan all its own: dry, oily, combination and, for a lucky few, normal. Before you can start a complexion-care program, you must know which skin you're in.

DRY skin feels tight when you wash it with soap and water. Dry and rough during the day, it tends to have a flaky redness around the nose, cheeks, and forehead. It chaps in the winter and burns in the summer.

Dry skin can also be sensitive; this means it develops a rash or allergic reaction from certain products or cosmetics. It can be equally sensitive to creams or astringents.

OILY skin has a shine that gets worse during the day. It can feel greasy and uncomfortable; if you run your finger across your forehead, you can see the oil on your hand. The extra oils can clog the pores of your skin and create blackheads and blemishes,

15

sometimes acne. These pores are noticeable if they're enlarged.

Oily skin has one advantage: Because the oils keep skin soft and pliant, you won't get as many wrinkles as quickly as your dry-skinned friends.

COMBINATION skin means certain areas are *dry*, usually the cheeks and neck, and others are *oily*, usually the forehead, nose, and chin, which form a shape like a "T" that is called the *T-zone*.

I have a combination complexion. Like me, you'll have to keep the T-zone free of oil as you keep the other areas lubricated.

NORMAL skin seems perfect—no signs of wrinkles, excess oil, or blemishes. Your skin feels soft, and its tone is even and clear. If you're the one lucky girl in ten, remember that you still have to care for your skin to keep it looking healthy.

Your skin, whatever type, needs attention in the morning and at night, before you go to sleep. Follow the right complexion care plan for your skin type.

Complexion Care for Dry Skin

The key word is *lubrication*. Dry skin needs to be kept moist and soft to keep it looking fresh and healthy. Follow these steps:

In the morning:

1. Wash your hands and splash your face with warm water.

2. Use a *glycerine* or *moisturizing soap* to make a rich lather on your face. With your fingertips, gently massage skin with the suds. Rinse with splashes of warm water for one minute, until all traces of soap are gone.

3. Pat your face dry and use a toner like *rosewater* or an *alcohol-free freshener* to stimulate your complexion. Apply it with a cotton ball.

4. Again with fingertips, apply a *nourishing moisturizer*, with emollients like mineral oil but not animal fats such as lanolin,

16

and humectants which seal in your skin's own moisture. If your skin is *very* dry, apply just mineral oil instead, sparingly, and blot with a tissue. You're ready to apply makeup!

In the evening:

If you wear makeup, remove it with a *cleansing cream* or *milky liquid cleanser* that dissolves impurities and is wiped off with tissue or rinsed with warm water. Follow with the four morning steps. If your skin is very dry, you might apply a *heavier cream* instead of a moisturizer. Leave it on for twenty minutes and blot off any that remains with a tissue so you don't wake up with a greasy pillow!

Once a week:

Try giving yourself a complete facial at home, using a recipe you can mix yourself in the kitchen. It's a lot of fun for you and a treat for your skin.

First, pin back your hair. Now remove makeup and superficial dirt with your cleanser. To open pores and release embedded dirt, steam your skin by applying a very hot washcloth to your face or by holding your head over a basin filled with boiling water. (Hold a towel over your head like a tent to contain the steam.) Next, wash with your special soap and water. Pat your face gently with a clean towel and apply this *face mask* for dry skin. Mix a ¼ cup of natural honey with ¼ cup oatmeal. Add just enough cleansing cream or liquid to blend and apply more easily (it's sticky!). Relax with your feet raised for twenty minutes. Now rinse it off, first with warm and then cool water. Finish your facial by applying rosewater and your moisturizer. If you're going out afterward, apply makeup. (This facial gives your skin a special glow for special occasions.)

You can alternate between this mask and a store-bought one. Look for the cream-based kind that moisturizes and nourishes and is rinsed, not peeled, off. (Peeling masks often dry skin further.)

Complexion Care for Oily Skin

The key word is *clean*. You want to check the oily secretions of your skin to keep it looking oil-free and clean. Follow these simple steps:

In the morning:
1. Wash your hands and splash your face with warm water.
2. Use an *antibacterial soap* to make a rich lather on your face. With fingertips, gently massage your skin with the suds for two or three minutes. Rinse for another minute with splashes of first warm then cool water to close the pores.
3. Pat your face dry with a clean towel and apply an alcohol-based toner called *astringent* with a cotton ball. This will stimulate your complexion and further close the pores.
4. With fingertips, apply a nourishing *moisturizer under the eyes only* to keep this delicate area soft. Now you're ready for makeup.

In the evening:
If you wear makeup, remove it with *cleansing liquid* or your astringent. Follow this with the four morning steps.

During the day:
If your skin is very oily, in the late morning and again in the afternoon you might want to remove oil excess by blotting with premoistened towelettes or by removing makeup (except around the eyes) with your astringent and cotton balls. Carry a purse-size plastic bottle of it with you. Afterward, you'll only have to reapply your blusher (and foundation, if you use it) but not your eye makeup.

Once a week:
Give yourself a complete facial at home, using a recipe you can mix in the kitchen. It's good for your skin and fun for you.
First, pin back your hair. Now remove makeup and superficial dirt with liquid cleanser or astringent. To open pores and release embedded dirt and oils, steam your skin by applying a very hot washcloth to your face or by holding your face over a basin filled

with boiling water. (Hold a towel over your head like a tent to contain the steam.) Next, wash your face with soap and water as directed. Pat your face gently with a clean towel and apply this *face mask* for oily skin:

Mix ¼ cup of coarsely ground almonds with ¼ cup of scrubbing grains (you can buy these at any beauty-care department). Add a small amount of lather from your soap to make it into a paste that's easy to apply.

Relax with your feet raised for extra comfort. After twenty minutes, rinse off the mask with cool water. Finish your facial by applying astringent and a dab of moisturizer under your eyes. If you're going out afterward, you can apply makeup now. (This facial gives your skin a special glow for special occasions.)

You can alternate between this mask and a store-bought one. Look for a dry mud mask that you apply by mixing with water. It has both drying and healing properties to help oily skin.

Complexion Care for Combination Skin

The key word is *balance*. You really have two different skin types, and each one needs its own kind of care. If it sounds like a lot of work, it actually isn't. I have combination skin: slightly dry on my cheeks, slightly oily on my nose and chin (and an occasional breakout, too!). In fact, most girls have this not very "winning combination." To balance the two, combine dry skin care with oily skin care on the appropriate areas.

In the morning:
1. Wash your hands and splash your face with warm water.
2. Use a nongreasy *milky cleanser* that is rinsed off with water. Massage it on your face and rinse for one minute.
3. Pat your face with a clean towel and, with a cotton ball, apply *astringent* to the T-zone. Apply *rosewater* or an *alcohol-free freshener* to the other areas.
4. Apply a *light moisturizer* all over, unless the T-zone is very oily. If so, apply it only to the dry areas. Now you can apply your makeup.

In the evening:

If you wear makeup, remove it with *cleansing cream* which dissolves the impurities and is wiped off with tissue. If your T-zone or nose is very oily, use astringent to cleanse. Now follow all the morning steps. If you'd rather use soap than the milky cleanser, try a clear *glycerine* bar that won't dry your skin. If the dry areas of your face are *very* dry, apply a *heavier cream* instead of moisturizer and leave it on for twenty minutes, then tissue off the excess; that's all the time it takes. Really.

Once a week:

One of the nicest parts of skin care is giving yourself a facial at home. It's not only simple and inexpensive to whip up a face mask, it also improves your complexion.

First, pin back your hair. Now remove your makeup as described in evening care. To open pores and release embedded dirt and oils, steam your skin by applying a very hot washcloth to your face or by holding your face over a basin you've filled with boiling water. (Drape a towel over your head like a tent to contain the steam.) Next, wash your face with milky cleanser mixed with a handful of *scrubbing grains*. Pat your face dry with a clean towel and apply half the recipe for the oily skin face mask on page 19 to the T-zone and half the recipe for the dry skin face mask on page 17 to the dry areas. Relax with your feet raised for extra comfort. After twenty minutes, rinse off the masks with first warm then cool water. Finish your facial by applying astringent to the oily areas and rosewater to those that are dry, followed by moisturizer, especially under your eyes. If you're going out afterward, you can apply your makeup now. (This facial gives your skin a special glow for special occasions.)

You can use store-bought masks as well as these homemade ones. Be sure that you buy one for dry skin and another for oily skin (they'll each last twice as long) and apply them to the appropriate areas.

Complexion Care for Normal Skin

If you've been blessed with near-perfect skin that never has any problems or complaints, you can probably get away without caring for it much. But if you do take a few minutes for the right kind of care, you can prevent any problems that might surprise you later.

Treat your skin to the complexion care described for dry skin. Astringents, used for oily skin, can dry out normal skin. But always use a *light moisturizer* and a *light milky liquid* cleanser —you don't need heavy creams. There's a chance that your nose might get shiny often (the nose secretes more oil than any other part of your face); if this happens to you, apply *astringent* lightly, with a cotton ball, instead of moisturizer on this area *only*.

Skin care doesn't stop with cleansing twice a day. Both your skin and body will benefit from these five rules:

1. *Eat a well-balanced diet of fresh foods.*

Your skin is nourished from the beauty products you apply on the outside, but it is equally nourished from inside with the foods you eat. Fresh fruits and vegetables, eaten raw or mixed in salads; lean meats, poultry, and fish; whole grains like bran cereal, unprocessed whole wheat bread, and wheat germ give your skin the healthy nutrients it needs to stay clear and shining. These foods also give you vitamins that keep your body functioning and doing the hundreds of little jobs that add up to a healthy you.

Some nutritionists now say that fried foods, chocolates, and sodas (sugary foods) don't create a bad complexion. But they don't help it either. These foods have hardly any nutritious value, and that means they are *not* healthy. Next time you want a glass of soda, try juice instead. You'll be surprised at how good it tastes!

2. *Get plenty of fresh air and exercise.*

When my family and I are on tour, working long hours and performing in smoke-filled rooms and theaters, I can feel the side effects, emotionally and physically. Exercising increases circulation; that's important because your blood feeds your skin and exercise gets it moving. Fresh air brings oxygen to your blood and your complexion; that nourishes it, too.

I get a lot of exercise during dance rehearsals every week while we prepare for our television show. When I'm not doing that, I love to take long, lively walks. An Osmond family game of touch football is terrific, too—if you have eight brothers! The next time you have Phys.Ed. at school, make a special effort at enthusiasm. Join a varsity team or simply ride your bike home from school instead of taking the bus. You'll look better and feel healthier in just a few weeks.

3. *Get a good night's sleep.*

Rest is important. A clear skin is one of the benefits of a calm, relaxed personality. I don't mean that you should stop having fun. Just be sure that you get the right amount of sleep every night.

Junior high and especially high school can provide some of the most exciting times in your life, but these years can also be a time of stress. You have to pass an especially hard test; you wonder when you'll have your first date; you don't think you'll ever be as popular as your friend Wendy. You may not think it's true at first, but these worries can ruin your complexion, as well as your whole semester, if you let them.

Stress can make an oily skin oilier and may cause breakouts. It can make a dry skin wrinkle if you frown a lot. Don't let these things get you down. Relax and put your best self forward.

4. *Protect your complexion.*

There are many elements working against your skin: dirt and smoke in the air you breathe, pollution, even the sun. The best way to protect your skin is to take care of it. Use the right type of products for your skin and use them as directed. Your beauty applications work with your complexion to make it the best it can be.

I think it's necessary to guard against the sun. I don't hide from it all the time, but I try to tan in *moderation*. The sun dries your skin's oils and can make it rough (this may also happen to oily skin). If you have oily, combination, or normal skin, use a sunscreen to block out harmful rays and expose your face to the sun for no more than ten or fifteen minutes a day. If you have dry skin, use a tanning oil and sun for only five to ten minutes.

The delicate skin under your eyes needs an extra minute of care every day. Because we squint, smile, and laugh, this area is used a lot; yet it has almost no natural oil to lubricate it. A dab of mineral oil or cream will help keep it soft. Apply it sparingly and blot any excess, in the morning and before bed (this is for *all* skins).

5. *Treat your complexion with tender, loving care.*

In our teens, it's hard to believe that our skin's ever going to show "old age." But as early as our twenties, tiny lines or wrinkles can begin to show (even earlier if your skin's very dry!). That's why it's never too soon to give your skin the gentle attention it deserves.

When you're cleansing your face or applying makeup, always be gentle. Never rub harshly or pull at your skin; this can stretch it needlessly.

The products you choose should be mild formulations. The fewer ingredients the better, I think. Too many detergents and too many chemicals spell trouble. And artificial coloring isn't necessary either. One of my friends once experimented with an expensive face mask that was painted on and peeled off the skin. It came in bright colors like blue and purple. Well, purple's fine for my brother Donny's socks, but not for a product you put on your face. The dyes used in this formulation couldn't be good for your skin. If you're not going to be more choosy, you might as well apply glue and close up your pores altogether! *Read labels.*

I like to choose a line of products brought out by the same company. A cleanser, a toner, and a moisturizer made to work with each other will give you better results than three products picked at random. But no system you choose has to be expensive. It's not always the quality of the ingredients that determines the price of a product but the amount of money spent in advertising and packaging!

Special Beauty Problems That Need Special Care

TROUBLED SKIN can mean anything from an occasional blemish or pimple to blackheads or breakouts. A skin with these problems is an oily skin, or at least partly oily. If you have a combination skin, you might have an occasional breakout on your chin or nose, like I do, or even on your forehead. Take all the right steps for oily skin: Keep it clean, use astringents to remove oil that rises to the surface, steam your face *every night* to open pores and release oils and blackheads, and follow with a *scrubbing grain* bath to help clear the pores. Before bed, reapply your astringent and never use oils, creams or moisturizers except under your eyes, if this delicate skin feels dry.

If you develop the kind of blemish that lies under the skin and feels sore a day or two before you see the oily accumulation on the surface, applying a hot washcloth or steaming your face will help it surface faster. Don't force it by squeezing or you'll break the skin and cause a scab and possibly a scar. It should ease out of the pore during the grain scrub. Afterward, dot it with calamine lotion for fast healing.

If your blemishes are severe or very complicated by reddened skin and pus, don't try to treat it yourself. A dermatologist can help clear the problem much more quickly. The worst thing you can do is try to hide it under globs of makeup or concealing cream. If you or your family doesn't know of a good dermatologist, ask your school doctor or nurse, or your family doctor. And always remember that there are more girls and guys who have blemishes at this time in their lives than there are those who don't.

While you're waiting for the blemishes to clear up, check your diet. Have you been eating fresh, healthful foods? Drinking lots of water—six to ten glasses a day—will help flush your body of toxins and other substances that could be aggravating your oily skin. Also, don't let the breakout get you down or tense. I know that's not so easy to do, but keeping your sense of humor about it will help. Stress and worry can actually make the oil glands produce more oil—something you don't want!

SENSITIVE SKIN can show itself at any time, and on almost any skin. You might get a blemish or a rash or just a few red blotches. If it's an allergic reaction, a certain food or a new beauty product may be the culprit. Check to see if you've used something new or maybe borrowed something from a friend. Creams especially can cause a reaction on sensitive skin. So do perfumed products and products that have scent added, like a depilatory. That doesn't mean you're allergic to perfume, but you should suspect everything until you locate the troublemaker.

When buying new products, choose those that are hypoallergenic or formulated for sensitive skin. (Always throw out a product that you know has caused a bad reaction on your skin; you'll be saving in the long run, even though it seems like wasted money now.)

FRECKLES are fun. Girls with freckles usually don't have problem skins. When all your friends have lost their tans, yours is still built-in. If your freckles are the kind that come out after you've been in the sun (and if you don't like them), protect your face with a sun block and a pretty, large straw hat. Once they're out, don't try to cover them. That only looks obvious, and on their own, they're really not as noticeable as you might think.

MOLES are usually called "beauty marks" for a reason—they are a part of your beauty personality. Look at all the actresses

PHOTOCRAFT

25

who have made one their trademark. You can even accent yours with an eyeliner pencil, as I do. Of course, if you feel that yours will always be a mole, you can ask your doctor about having it removed. If it's only a slight discoloration, you might be able to hide it with a cover stick, a creamy makeup in the color of your skin tone. (This also works with small scars.) Never tweeze hair growing from a mole; snip it with manicure-sized scissors.

A DULL COMPLEXION can be caused by poor diet and lack of exercise or sleep. Makeup isn't the best answer. Becoming more active and healthy is. You can also wake up your complexion by using scrubbing grains mixed with a little soap lather or milky cleanser twice a week. (I like the kind that contains ground almonds, though you should use a brand labeled for your skin type.) Massage the mixture into your skin with your fingertips. Do this for a full minute and rinse with cool water. You can see and feel your face tingle. The grains stimulate the skin by bringing blood to the surface and cleansing the pores of dirt and dead skin cells that make it look dull. It's terrific!

BROKEN CAPILLARIES are small blood vessels that appear on the surface of skin, making it look ruddy. The best way to avoid this is to treat your skin gently. Never rub or pull, as these actions can cause the vessel to break. If you should get a broken capillary, you can camouflage it with the cover stick. (It can be removed by a dermatologist, but that may cost a lot of money.)

BEAUTY TOOLS FOR COMPLEXION CARE

In addition to the beauty products mentioned in the different skin-care sections, every girl should have these helpers:

- Cotton balls
- Cotton facial tissues
- Clean, white face or hand towels
- Covered holder for your soap
- Clean basin or bathroom sink for a fresh start every morning and evening

With a healthy, shining complexion, you'll be ready for makeup when that special time comes.

3.

The Beauty Part:
The Fun of Makeup

I LOVE MAKEUP—makeup's fun. And it's great when you can see an instant improvement in your looks. It's also a challenge, especially when you know enough to share it with your friends. For me, experimenting with cosmetics is a getaway from work, even though makeup is part of performing (a behind-the-scenes part, that is).

I remember watching my mother put on makeup. I was fascinated . . . and eager to try it myself. I began playing with makeup at a very early age. I tried on my first pair of false eyelashes when I was seven years old! (I think that false eyelashes are just for playing at grownup because they look very artificial. I don't recommend them for most girls at seventeen or twenty-seven any more than at seven, unless you're appearing on stage or television. If I wear them in concert, it's so that the people in the balcony can see my eyes!)

Even though I didn't start performing until I was in my teens, my family was in show business many years before that. I would investigate the makeup rooms backstage and at the television studios. I loved the pretty packaging and all the different colors of lipstick and eyeshadow. At home, I would put on so much that my mother would remind me that I couldn't leave the house until it was all washed off.

At first, you want to use as much makeup as you can. It's all so new, you just can't seem to try it fast enough. But as you learn the techniques of makeup, you understand that you look your best with the *least* amount you apply. Soft little touches work together to create the total look. It's never one drastic line of color; it's a combination of the little ones, and knowing where to put them.

The shape of your face changes as you get older. Baby fat doesn't belong just to babies. I found that out when we first began doing "The Donny and Marie Show." I didn't have any cheekbones; my face was as round as a circle. But as I lost weight, a little at a time, and as my features became more defined each year, my makeup changed accordingly. The first things I used were lip gloss, a dab of blusher, and a little mascara on the tips of the lashes. And until you start dating, when you're sixteen or so, that's really all you need too. My brothers all agree that nothing looks worse on a young girl than globs of makeup. Guys like us to look pretty, but in a natural way. When your skin is fresh and healthy, you don't need foundation or face powder to clog your pores. And heavy eye makeup, applied before you really learn how, can make you look like you have two black eyes.

I trust my mother, so I listened to her advice, but lots of girls won't believe something you tell them until they try it themselves. I think that experimenting on your own is terrific. There's no greater teacher, no better way to learn about your own features and how to accent them properly.

Most of my knowledge has been gained by watching some of show business's greatest makeup artists and hairdressers at work in television, movie, and photography studios. Way Bandy has "designed" my face three times, and each time he has made me look totally different. That's creativity! But you can be your own makeup artist, if you take the time to study your subject: your features. It's also helpful to study makeup and fashion magazines. Each new look that comes along may not be right for you, but you'll learn what does, as well as what doesn't, look good. You may also learn new ways to apply your favorite cosmetics and read about new colors and improvements that have been made. I'm not always as on top of the makeup world as I'd like to be. Some weeks, I get too bogged down with movie and television scripts to enjoy reading magazines. Then, when I have a weekend off, I catch up by reading as many as I can. If you've got a lot of studies and school activities that are too important to neglect, set aside a special hour or two on a Saturday and do your investigating then.

Every girl can be pretty if she takes care of herself and finds out how best to apply makeup to make the most of her features —her eyes, her mouth, her cheekbones. When girls say to me, "But I don't have your bone structure . . . ," I say, "Baloney!

Look at any of today's beauties and you'll see that each one has created her own kind of beauty and style."

I have features that I'd like to change, but I can't. So instead of getting upset, I work to improve them. For instance, when I get tired, I have a tendency to retain water, and that makes my eyes and face puffy. Camouflaging the puffiness is part of my makeup routine. I've learned how to accent my cheeks with blush and how to use makeup to make my nose look more chiseled. My upper lip needs definition, so I line it with a lip pencil before applying gloss or lipstick. I have a technique that opens my eyes and makes them appear larger. These are only some of the "little touches" I told you about before.

No matter what your bone structure, once you learn to work with it, you can be pretty too. Minimize your "flaws" and make the most of your assets. Everyone's face is different, from the shape of the face to the eyes, the nose, the mouth. That's why I can only give you ideas and tips on what I've learned. You have the fun of personalizing it!

There is one rule that applies to all of us. Your makeup has to look natural. Maybe you'll want to use only a little—some girls look better with less. But there are also girls whose features need makeup to define and enhance them. To find what works best for you, you have to try everything. Be experimental! Discard items that don't improve your looks. For example, there are girls who don't look pretty with colored eye shadow; it closes their eyes instead of opening them. They should use just a hint of blusher under the eyebrows.

Beauty Helpers

Here's a list of the basic cosmetics and tools you'll want to try. Not everyone needs all of them. Maybe you're not ready for foundation yet. Skip over that section to the one on eyes. Maybe you're just starting to wear lipstick; you can turn to that section now and read through the others later, as you need them. Even though I'm not wild about false eyelashes, I've included them here as a reference; you might need to call on them for an extra-special occasion, like a school performance. Girls with blond or red hair and very light eyelashes might need them more frequently but not until after high school. They give a formal look that's just not right for English Lit. class! (Try multiple applications of mascara until your mom gives her okay.)

THE COSMETIC	ITS BEST APPLICATION TOOL
Foundation	Makeup sponge
Cover stick	Narrow slant-edged sable-hair brush
Translucent face powder	A large cotton ball
Eye shadow:	
—powdered	Straight-edged sable-hair brush
—cream	
—pencils	
Mascara, wand-type	
Eyeliner:	
—cake	Thin sable-hair brush
—pencil	
False eyelashes and adhesive	Tweezers
Eyebrow pencil	
Blusher:	
—powdered	Bushy sable-hair brush
—cream	
Lipliner pencil	
Lip gloss	A narrow square-edged brush
Lipstick	A narrow square-edged brush

BEAUTY TOOLS

- Eyelash curler, with clean rubber strip
- Petroleum jelly, to lubricate lashes
- Baby powder, to thicken lashes in between coats of mascara
- Mustache wax, to tame thick, unruly eyebrows
- Sponge-tipped shadow brush, to smudge shadows and liner
- Cotton swabs and tissues, to smudge and blot as needed
- Hand-held mirror, to double-check your makeup
- Plant mister or extra makeup sponge, to damp-set makeup

At first, that list might seem long, but you don't need everything at once. Start slowly and build your cosmetic wardrobe as you can.

Whether you're experimenting (which you should do *before* you wear makeup outside your room) or applying it for the day, the area you work in should be well organized. There's nothing more nerve-racking than being in the middle of putting on your eyeshadow and not being able to find the right brush. Try covering a large shoebox with pretty wrapping paper and keeping all your items inside it. If you have a bigger budget, you can buy a plastic or lucite tray with individual compartments for each cosmetic.

Dressing room lights are very bold. They help you scrutinize your makeup. But they're expensive. At home, I apply my makeup at a small dressing table that's placed in front of a window. Natural daylight is the most severe critic, but if your makeup looks correct in that light, you'll probably look your best in all lights. You can double-check by using the bathroom mirror. This light is similar to what is used in buildings, movie theaters, and restaurants. If you have to apply your makeup in the bathroom, check it in a hand mirror at any light-giving window afterward. Make all the touch-ups you need there.

They key to applying great-looking makeup is getting a clean, fresh start. Have you prepared your skin as described in the last chapter? The last step is to apply your moisturizer all over if your skin is dry, or just your astringent if your skin is oily. There are nine different makeup items on my list. All or in any combination add up to a more beautiful you.

1. FOUNDATION

Foundation is a flesh-colored liquid or cream that covers your skin's imperfections and smoothes out uneven skin tones. Depending on the type you choose, it can act as a treatment for sensitive, oily, or combination skin, or it can nourish dry skin. Many women rely on it, but I don't think it should be one of the first cosmetics you buy. (However, when you do use it, it's the first thing you apply.) Until you reach "a certain age," young skin is attractive enough on its own. The early use of foundation often causes skin problems. For very troubled complexions, there are extra-medicated lotions that cover like a foundation and are usually available only with a prescription; ask your doctor about this alternative.

Once you do decide to wear foundation, it's important that

you choose the right one for your skin type and your skin tone:

If you have oily, combination, or sensitive skin, choose a water-based liquid foundation.

If you have dry skin, choose a creamy liquid or cream-based foundation. Oil-based foundations aren't good for any skin. They are heavy products that can cake on your face as well as clog pores.

The foundation's color should match the overall tone of your skin. You can't get an instant tan with foundation; it won't look right.

If your skin is pale, look for a shade that has rosy highlights to give you a brighter glow.

If your skin is rosy or ruddy, look for a shade that has beige highlights to balance your skin tone.

If your skin is sallow or yellow or if it has an olive cast, look for a shade that has brown, not gold or beige highlights.

Always test the shade on the skin of your face, not on your hand or wrist which is not at all the same skin tone. The color should blend into the skin along your jawline, into the top of your throat and neck so that you don't have to bring it too far down.

Five steps to a better foundation application:
• Foundation must be applied with a light hand for natural cov-

PHOTOCRAFT

erage. In the palm of your hand, dilute it with a little water and moisturizer (if your skin's not oily) and then apply it with your sponge or fingertips. Place one dot on each cheek, one each on forehead and chin and, with the sponge, stroke it upward and outward.

- If you need extra coverage, apply *two* light coats instead of one heavy one. Make sure the first is set before you apply the second.
- To look and feel right, foundation must be expertly blended. Check to see that there are no lines to show where the foundation starts and stops.
- As you reach the jawline, begin to taper off the foundation so that you don't have to cover your neck—this saves laundry time.
- After you've applied the foundation, take a clean sponge and dampen it with cold water. Wring it out completely and pat your face to set the color and remove any excess. You can also mist your face lightly, instead, and blot with a tissue.

If you're not happy with the color you've selected, or any others available, you can blend two different shades to make your own. Use testers at cosmetics counters and blend a few drops of one shade with a few drops of another, a little darker or lighter, depending on what you need. Test it on your face. If it's not quite right, try it again, changing the proportions of the two shades until you mix the right combination. Buy both—they'll last twice as long as one bottle so you're not spending any extra money. You can mix the colors as you need them or blend a batch in a clean, purse-size plastic bottle.

2. COVER STICK (HIGHLIGHTER)

Sometimes, foundation isn't enough to conceal a small scar, discoloration under the eyes, or an occasional blemish. Use in cases of emergency only; the creamy emollients in a cover product can add oiliness to an already troubled skin. I use a light cover stick (without any pearlescence that can look artificial and cause irritation) when I need to look perfect but haven't gotten as much sleep as I need. Though it's handy, remember that this cosmetic is not a substitute for proper skin care and rest.

PHOTOCRAFT

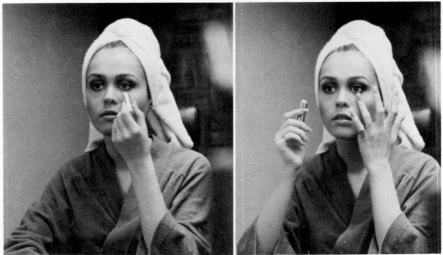

Five steps to a better cover stick application:
- Choose a concealer that is the same shade as your skin or only one shade lighter. Any more than this and it looks phony.
- Dot the product over the area to be covered with a fingertip or the slant-edged sable brush and blend it gently into your foundation at the edges. If you don't wear foundation, make sure that the cover stick blends into your skin perfectly; it shouldn't look like a big white dot!
- If your skin's not oily, you can use cover stick instead of foundation to blend skin tones in limited areas, such as above the upper lip, around the nostrils, and anywhere that is darkened by natural shadows.
- Very effective for hiding dark circles under the eyes, cover stick must be applied as gently as possible to avoid stretching and pulling this delicate skin.
- You can also use a concealer as a highlighter, at the top of your cheekbones, the inner corner of the eyes (to make them appear wider apart), and just under the arch of the brows. Blend it in thoroughly so that it adds shine, not a whitish streak.

3. TRANSLUCENT FACE POWDER

Sheer talc will cut down on shine—on your forehead, your

chin, your nose—but used properly, it won't leave a powdery film on your face. If you don't use foundation, you might want to apply translucent powder over your moisturizer or astringent to act as a base for your blusher.

Choose translucent powder in a shade that's closest to your skin color. Usually, you can pick from three tones: light, medium, and dark. The powder doesn't add color, just a smooth finish.

Five steps to a better powder application:
- Choose loose powder, not the pressed kind that contains oil and can cake in the compact.
- Apply the powder with a bushy sable brush or a large cotton ball. Dip it into the powder and tap or shake off the excess. Then lightly brush it on the shiny areas (or all over, if you like). With a clean piece of cotton, whisk off any excess.
- Check to be sure there aren't any traces in your hair or on your clothes.
- You can lightly powder your eyelashes to help hold the mascara later, but brush out any that falls into your brows.
- If your skin is very oily, carry facial tissues or linens with you during the day and blot off excess oil before you reapply powder. Use it sparingly so that it doesn't get heavy and cake with the oil.

4. EYE SHADOW

I love to experiment with eye shadows; sometimes I blend my own mix to coordinate with an outfit I'm wearing (it's really not necessary, but it's fun!). I'm able to do my own makeup when I'm on tour with my family. I've learned that for stage appearances, you can exaggerate your makeup—there's no camera to catch every little flaw. But when I'm appearing on television, I work with a fantastic makeup man. Bob and I experiment together, and I learn what works best for the camera. Still, I've found that the most important makeup is the one I do for every day. How you play up your eyes really determines the whole effect of your makeup because when you talk to people, they always look at your eyes, not at your mouth or cheeks. And that's why the cosmetics you select for your eyes have to be chosen with extra care.

Wearing the wrong color eye shadow is one of the most frequently made mistakes. Since this is one of the first items you'll be wearing, you should start off on the right track. Eye *shadow* means just that, a delicate accent for your eyes, not a hard line of bright color. There are many techniques for applying shadow that can give the illusion of bigger, brighter eyes. And no matter what your eye color, they all call for subtle tones.

Five steps to choosing the right eye shadow:
- Look closely at your eyes. What colors do you see in the iris? If there are gray, green, yellow, gold, or lavender highlights, choose a subtle shadow in one of these shades to complement the overall color of your eye, not to match it.
- Don't choose strong bright colors like cornflower blue, kelly green, purple, or any with irridescence which can irritate and dry out the tender skin of the eyelids.
- Choose two tones of the same shade, such as a pale lavender and a deeper lavender, a beige and a deeper tone with more brown highlights, a dove gray and a charcoal. Two variations of the same shade can be applied in a variety of ways to enhance the eye.
- Neutral shades of beige, bisque, and earth can enhance eyes that aren't enhanced by more obvious colors. Certain shades of blush work well, too.
- When you're buying shadows, make sure you have the proper tools to work with: sable brushes for applying, sponge-tipped ones or cotton swabs for smudging and softening the effect.

Eye shadows come in different forms: creams, liquids, pencils, and powdered—my favorite. You have a lot more control over the degree of color, and unlike creams and soft pencils, powdered shadow doesn't get easily creased in the middle of your eyelids.

Five steps to a better shadow application:
- Use shadow to make your eyes look wide set. Apply a lighter variation of the basic shade on the inner half of the lid. Intensify the color on the outer half, blending well in the center so that the change in color is gradual.
- Use shadow to make your eyes look larger and to make the brow bone recede. Apply a light shadow color (example: fawn)

on the entire lid. Place a darker version (example: mocha brown) over this, from the crease in the middle of the lid to the eyebrows. The darker color minimizes the bone; the light one makes the eyes more prominent.

- When you're working with two shades, you can use the darker one subtly to line the eye, close to the roots of the upper and lower lashes. This is a softer look than conventional black eyeliner. You might try a charcoal gray for this, too; it's easier to blend and smudge than black (see the steps on eyeliner later on).
- If you want to use only a hint of shadow, apply it very close to the roots of the upper lashes, concentrating it on the outer half of the lid. To make eyes seem larger, extend it to the outer corner and under the lower lashes as well.
- Concentrate the color on the outer half of the upper and lower eyelids close to the lash roots. This makes the eyes appear wider apart. Do the same with liner and mascara.

Special tips:

If you don't wear foundation, powder eyes lightly before you apply shadow; this gives shadow a base to cling to.

If you like the fun and ease of shadow pencils, be sure you have the right size sharpener for them (the fatter pencils need a

37

super-sized one) and make sure the points are good before you start the application.

Keep up on the newest shadow colors and experiment with shades like mauve, plum, berry, teal, heather, and spice.

5. EYELINER

Used in a new and exciting way, this cosmetic can define your eyes softly. Eyeliner is no longer a hard black line. It's a smudged look that adds a little magic, not a black eye! Try one of the newer liner pencils or, for more control and a thinner line, use a liner cake and a thin-pointed sable brush. (If you use cake mascara, you may also use this as eyeliner; you won't need two separate products.)

Five steps to a better liner application:
- Dot the eyeliner close to the roots of your lashes; don't paint it on in a straight line. With a moist cotton swab, smudge the dots lightly to add fullness at the base of the lashes. This technique will define your eyes and make your lashes look longer.

- If you concentrate the dots at the outer half of both the top and bottom lids, you'll really bring your eyes into prominence.
- If you don't like using black liner, which can be hard to handle until you gain some more experience, practice with a medium or charcoal gray color. It's softer.
- To open eyes and add depth, don't line the upper lid, but cover it with a light shadow. Now thinly line the bottom lid, just underneath the lash roots, with black or gray. Wear plenty of mascara, too.
- You can achieve an interesting effect by lining the inner rim of the lower lid with a teal blue pencil, especially nice if you have blue eyes. Green eyes? Use a light forest green. Brown eyes should try lining with a dark brown or black pencil.

6. MASCARA

The mysterious look you can have when you use mascara has nearly every girl counting the days until she can try it. While you're waiting, try applying a little petroleum jelly to your lashes for lubrication; it helps them stay in condition and look richer. Another way to play up your lashes is to use an eyelash curler. Slip the upper lashes in the slit and press down three or four times in about five seconds, tightly squeezing the curler. The curled lashes are more visible and look longer, too. Always use

PHOTOCRAFT

the curler before mascara and be sure the rubber strip on the curler is clean and in good condition. It can be replaced when it wears out.

When you're ready to wear mascara, it's best to invest in two kinds, a conditioning mascara and a lash-lengthening one (the first acts as a foundation or base for the second one) in brown or black. They can be either the wand type or a cake and brush. Before you start, there's one other item you need. Ask your father or brother to look in his electric razor kit for the little wire brush that's meant to clean the razor (your father may not use it anyway!). *You* can use it to separate your lashes in between coats of mascara, so that they don't get clumped together.

Five steps to a better mascara application:
- Dust your lashes lightly with face powder or baby talc (whichever is available).
- Apply the first coat of mascara, the conditioning one. Stroke it on from the roots to the tips, on the upper and underside of top and bottom lashes. Lashes are just like the hairs on your head and need pampering.
- Before the mascara dries completely, use the wire brush to separate lashes. Now repowder them.
- Apply the second coat of mascara, the lengthening one. Again use the brush to separate any clumps.
- Check in your mirror to see if there are any mascara flakes

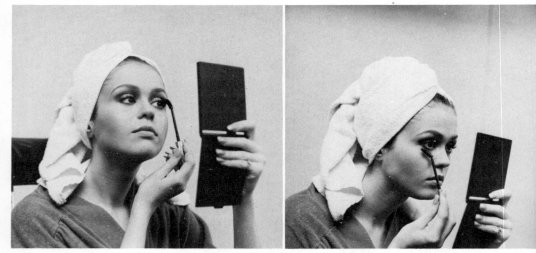

PHOTOCRAFT

where they shouldn't be. Use a moistened cotton swab to remove them. Now look at your lashes. If they need another coat of mascara, apply it.

Taking off your mascara is almost as important as applying it. I know that many girls sleep with it on, but I don't think that's a good idea. I've always made it a point to remove my mascara (and all other makeup) at night, right before I do the evening cleansing of my skin. If there's anything on my lashes while I sleep, it's petroleum jelly to keep them lubricated.

If it's not removed, mascara can dry out lashes and cause them to fall out. You don't need an expensive product to remove it. Baby oil, petroleum jelly, or plain hot water and a little soap on the tip of a cotton swab will do the trick. Stroke the swab along the length of your lashes from the roots to the tips, twirling it to remove the makeup.

By accident, I found that the tannic acid in tea bags is good for lashes, too. When I'm overtired and my eyelids are puffy, I place a warm moist tea bag on each closed lid to ease the swelling. After I had done this a few times one week, I noticed the positive results on my lashes and my eyebrows. At one time, the lashes were so long I didn't need false ones, even on television.

Speaking of false lashes . . . You already know that I think they're just plain ridiculous during the day. I wear them while I'm performing because my eyes need to reach the audience. But because I know there will be a special and appropriate time when you'll want to wear them, I'll tell you how I learned to use them.

To add depth and make my eyes less round, I often apply individual lashes on the outer corners of my upper lids. Other times, when I need a fuller, longer look, I use skinnies—eight lashes on a strip. (They look like the false lashes made for lower lids which don't really need them.)

After putting a tiny bit of surgical glue or adhesive on the tip of the individuals or along the band of the skinnies, I pick them up with tweezers and center them at the lashline with a fingertip. It's really a hit-and-miss experiment at first, and you'll need lots of time to practice. Carefully applied, lashes can enhance your eyes and give them a little oomph. Badly applied, they can ruin your look. *Practice*.

7. EYEBROW MAKEUP

Your eyebrows are the frames for your eyes but shouldn't themselves attract attention. They should complement your eyes, not compete with them. Bushy, unruly eyebrows can really get in the way of your looking your best; they can be thinned with tweezers and/or lightened with hair bleach (I'll tell you how in chapter 5). But don't be so quick to reach for the tweezers if your brows are naturally well shaped. Once you start you can never stop, because the hairs grow back at different speeds so it's hard to get a brand-new start.

To tame your eyebrows, start by brushing them with an eyebrow brush; it looks like a miniature toothbrush, shaped perfectly for your brows. Brush them straight up and then use the side of the brush to coax them back into line.

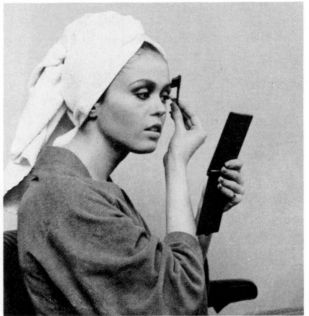

PHOTOCRAFT

If the brush isn't enough, you can use a little petroleum jelly on the bristles; it will help soften and curb hairs as you brush. For impossible hairs, use a little mustache wax in the same manner.

42

Tweezing shapes the brows for you, but they might still need filling in. Maybe you tweezed a few too many hairs; maybe the thin, tapered part after the arch needs pencil help; maybe they're not dark enough; maybe they need to be lightened. You can handle this by working with eyebrow pencils.

PHOTOCRAFT

Five steps to a better eyebrow pencil application:
- Eyebrows should be a slightly lighter shade than your hair color. Choose a pencil that matches as closely as possible. Blonds and redheads will get the best results with gray and beige pencils.
- Use a pencil specifically designed for the eyebrows. A shadow pencil will have too fat a point. Make sure all your pencils are sharpened before you begin, or you'll have a smudged look where you don't want it.
- Fill in your brows with tiny, thin strokes. Try to simulate individual hairs. You can soften any hard lines by brushing twice with the brow brush afterward.
- Don't try to change the shape of your brows with the pencil only. You'll have to tweeze as well. (Tweezing is always done in the evening before bed, not before you go out because it can cause redness.)

43

- Like other features that come in pairs, the brows don't always match perfectly. That's natural, so don't spend too much time and worry trying to make them look identical.

For girls who wear glasses (like me!) . . .

It's no longer a beauty drawback to wear stylish frames that enhance your looks as they improve your vision. If you wear glasses, there are some special makeup tricks you can do to make your eyes as pretty as ever.

- The frames you select should line up with your eyebrows. That way you won't have two sets of frames for your eyes. Your brows are your best guide to the right size frame for your face. If they stick out above the frames, the frames are too small. If you can see the brows through the glass, the frames are too big. And they shouldn't come down any lower on your face than the top of your cheekbone.
- Glasses change the look of your makeup. Lenses for farsighted eyes tend to magnify them so keep eye makeup simple, not too much shadow and not too bright a color (try a warm shade, like a rosy brown); lenses for nearsighted eyes minimize them so brighten your eye shadow and extend it like an eyeliner, under your lower lashes at their roots. Don't forget your eyelash curler and mascara, if you wear it.
- All lenses emphasize shadows under your eyes. If you have these dark circles or if your skin is very transparent and shows tiny veins, camouflage them with your cover stick.
- To add a little glamor to eyes that are shaded by glasses, try one of the suggestions for wearing two shades of shadow in varying degrees of the same color.
- Mascara is especially important if you don't like wearing eye shadow. Three coats give you a lush look.

(See chapter 9 for more hints on choosing the right frames.)

8. BLUSHER

I think that blushers are great. We'd all like to look naturally healthy, but we can't always look like we've just taken a long walk in the country. Adding a little color to your cheeks can really brighten your complexion, but too strong a color in the wrong places can look like war paint!

If you're just starting to use rouge, try a powdered blusher. Gels and creams are fun, too (though only for *dry* skin), but you have more control with powder and it's good for all skins. If your skin is very dry, apply a moisturizer first, if you don't wear a nourishing foundation.

Once you get the hang of it, you can try other formats and play with different shades. One of the best makeup tricks I know is using two shades in the same family, one slightly darker than the other. The lighter shade goes on the top of your cheekbone, the darker blends into it at the bottom of the cheekbone for contour. It's a great look but only for the advanced makeup artist.

Finding the right shade of rouge and lipstick is an important consideration: first, because you want to achieve as real and believable a makeup as possible, and second, because your rouge is your guide to choosing the right lipstick. Lipstick and rouge must be compatible with each other and with your eye shadows. Can you imagine how peculiar it would look to wear an orangey shade of lipstick with a red rouge and lavender eye shadow? That's why it's a must to wear subtle shades of shadow and to coordinate all your makeup colors—this is a tricky business.

Generally, your rouge should come as close as possible to the skin tone of your natural blush, and your lipstick should be in the same family, about two shades deeper at the most. Take a look at your face, without rouge, after you've been exercising for ten minutes or after a walk in the cold winter weather. If you don't have time to wait for cold weather, rub an ice cube on one cheek only. Compare it to the other cheek. That's the color you want to look for.

There are four families of rouge: the pinks and reds, the mauves, and peaches, and the browns. The blusher you pick should have only highlights of one of these shades. It should never be a pure mauve (your cheeks will look purply frozen!), or a pure peach (you'll have an instant attack of jaundice!), or any other pure color. Only a subtle blend will be right for you. You might hear that one makeup artist uses one particular technique, another swears by his special method, a third uses browns and blue-reds. Well, most of the time, these people are trying to achieve a special look for their subject, probably for a professional appearance or photographic session, *not for every day.* Even the most famous fashion models wouldn't wear their "work face" in public.

Five steps to a better blusher application:
• The best place to apply blusher, on most faces, is the center of the cheekbone, midway between the nostril and the ear. Then blend it upward along the top of the bone. Be sure the blusher blends perfectly into your foundation, if you wear it, or into your skin itself, at the edges.

PHOTOCRAFT

• The best way to apply powdered blusher is with a bushy sable brush, not a powder puff. Stroke the brush on the cake, tap off the excess, and stroke it on your cheeks.
   The best way to apply cream blusher or rouge, for those with dry skin only, is with a cosmetic sponge, not with your fingers. (Fingertips can leave fingerprints!) The sponge helps the color glide on. Use the side edge of the sponge to blend in the color.
• You can blend your own blusher colors by mixing two shades. Creams blend easily in the palm of your hand. For powders, remove them from their containers and place in a bowl. Use the handle of a knife or a pestle to crush them. (If the new blusher you bought looks too dark of if you like the shade but

46

want it a little bit lighter, crush it and add some loose, translucent face powder until you get the results you want.)
- Though oily skin should use only powdered blusher, dry skin can use both powder and cream. Apply the cream first to give a hint of color and then contour or intensify with the powder. You can reapply powder later in the day when you see the color fading; it will intensify the cream all over again.

PHOTOCRAFT

- Use blusher to accent your temples, or the bridge of your nose (not the tip or you'll look like Rudolph the Red-Nosed Reindeer!), or your upper eyelids, under the arch of your brows if you don't wear shadow there.

9. LIPSTICK

I've saved the best for last. Though lipstick is probably the first cosmetic you've tried, it is applied after any and all others because it is the first to smudge and wear off.

I might have tried on my mother's favorite red the first time I experimented at home, but the first time I wore any out of the house, it was a clear gloss that added just a little shine. Dark or very bright lipstick can "age" you faster than any other cosmetic because it occupies a prominent place. My brothers told me to go easy with lipstick because it can look too obvious if you're not

PHOTOCRAFT

careful. I still like using gloss, but now it's the tinted kind that adds shine *and* color. Lip pencils are also fun to use; they give you a lot of control, too. Use the pencil point to outline and define your lips, especially the "M" shape of the two points of the upper lip. Then color in lightly with the pencil and finish with gloss to add shine. When you want to perfect your lipstick and have a little extra money, you can get a narrow, flat sable brush to apply the gloss (it's more precise than a fingertip).

A brush is the best way to apply lipstick from a tube. The color's more concentrated, so you want to be sure it goes on in the right places—start from the corners and blend the color over your lips. Oh—when you're using the brush, stroke it over the lipstick or gloss, from left to right, on both sides; never rub it into the lipstick. That ruins the cosmetic and gets the hairs of the brush out of whack. The rich color of tube lipstick is good for night makeup: Artificial lights drain the color from your face; a brighter lipstick will hold up longer.

Five steps to a better lipstick application:
• You can improve the shape of your mouth with lipstick, but

PHOTOCRAFT

you can't use it to paint on whatever shape you'd like to have. Your lips are three-dimensional and have two outlines, not just one. The smaller outline is their color, the second is their structure. Look closely and you'll see that there's a point where the color stops, but the shape of your lips extends a little farther. If your lips look too full, apply lipstick along the color outline. If they look too thin, apply lipstick along the structural outline.

- Use a lighter, softer color during the day when sunlight intensifies it. Use a brighter one at night when artificial lights drain color.
- To help lipstick or gloss last longer, powder lips first. You can use face powder if you have it, or plain baby talc.
- Practice dabbing on clear gloss with your pinkie. You can use it to refresh lip color during the day, even when you can't get to a mirror.
- Always check your teeth for any lip color that might have smeared before you give yourself the okay.

A little extra glamor: For a special date, use just a hint of gold

49

lipstick on the center of your lower lip. Then put a dab of it mixed with your regular gloss on your eyelids and at the very top of your cheeks to create a pretty look that ties these three together.

Your three makeup personalities

No matter how big or small your wardrobe is, it's probably divided into the three important aspects of your life: school or work, playtime and sports, special occasions like dates. Well, your makeup wardrobe should complement each. But unlike your clothes, you don't need a different set of makeup for each activity. All you have to do is combine the nine different choices in different ways. Let me show you what I mean.

During the day, whether you're at school or at work, your makeup should be conservative: a little blusher, a dab of mascara on the tips of your lashes, and some gloss.

On weekends or for after-school activities like ice-skating or taking a long walk, you might wear an even simpler makeup. If you're outdoors, you probably don't want or need any cosmetic blusher, but you must use your moisturizer to protect against the sun or wind. If you have oily skin, a light application of face powder is enough protection.

For dates and other special occasions like holiday outings and parties, you can experiment with all nine cosmetics, if you've started wearing them. Foundation gives you the base for a formal makeup; eye shadow adds excitement, so does eyeliner.

You can create your own combinations to suit every activity and mood. Just be sure you have enough time to wash it all off and start again if you've never tried one before. And after every makeup application, always check your work in the mirror and in good light. That way only you will know where your beauty begins.

If you're following me by chapter, by now you're probably wondering what to do with your hair. Somewhere in chapter 2, you pinned it up, and you're probably thinking that I've forgotten about it. Well, I haven't. Your hair can make an even bigger difference in your looks than makeup does. Just turn the page.

Use subtle shades of eye shadow. Blend a darker shade in the crease of the eyelid for drama and depth.

Pencil your brows with thin, light strokes—and never overtweeze!

Eyeliner goes on close to the upper and lower lashes. Smudge it for a soft, eye-opening look.

Apply two light coats of mascara, never one heavy coat, for lush, natural-looking lashes.

Cover stick is for dark circles—or any other small flaw you'd like to minimize. Apply gently!

Blusher belongs on your upper cheekbones. Blend it carefully with upward strokes.

Apply your foundation with a light hand and blend thoroughly for a natural glow.

Define your lips with a sharpened lip pencil, then fill in with a complementary shade of lipstick.

THE SPECIAL OCCASION FACE
Makeup you apply with skill . . . a fresh flower in your hair . . . confidence that shines from within . . . and you're all set for a special evening out!

4.

The Beauty Part:
Hair . . . Style It Right

YOUR HAIR CAN be your greatest asset, if you learn how to work with it as I did. Until Donny and I started to do our television series, I was happy to let my hair grow long, to wash it and set it in a flip and not think about it again. Sure, it looked nice, but it didn't enhance my features the way my short style does.

The best thing about your hair is that you can change it to any look you want (within reason, of course!). Sure, you can change your nose, but you can't change it back or wear it in six different styles. If you're really unhappy with your hair, you could even change its color (though I don't think you should until you can have a professional do it and can afford the upkeep). One of the most dramatic yet simple changes is in the style of your hair.

Getting the Right Haircut

Cutting your hair doesn't always mean making long hair short. That was the decision I made, but it's not right for everyone. I'm glad to have this chance to tell all the girls who have written to me that they want to have their hair cut just like mine that they *all* shouldn't. Lots of girls look cute with short hair, but lots of others don't. Don't forget about shoulder-length hair and long hair!

The style you choose depends on a lot of considerations: the size of your face and its different features, your body (its height and weight), how thick or thin your hair is, and whether its job is to enhance or, more importantly, to help camouflage your bone structure. There's more to a good haircut than a pair of scissors with a bowl as a guide!

When I was thirteen, I loved my long hair.

I love reading fashion and beauty magazines, but I don't always follow their advice to the letter. The styles they suggest for makeup, hair, and fashion are just that—suggestions, possibilities, ideas for you to use. A good hairdresser will be able to show you how a certain look can be adapted to your best advantage; that's why it's important to find someone to whom you can talk and in whom you have confidence. When I made that exciting trip to New York to have my hair cut by the famous stylist Suga, we both did a lot of talking and experimenting with different styles before the final cut. In fact, for about a day, I had a great shoulder-length style that he called "the dandelion." But the day after, we thought we should take the chance and go for the shorter length. It was less of a shock to give up my long hair gradually, and it's really worked well. In fact, my short hair has a lot more versatility, now that I know how to work with it.

(More about styling and changing your look with at-home settings later.)

No matter what length hair you have, if you have a good cut, you'll have great-looking hair. If you hair's thin or hard to manage, the right cut is even more necessary to build thickness or tame it naturally. Here are some ideas to consider when you're thinking of which new style to try.

If you have *thin* hair, a cut that's layered will add fullness. Short hair will give you bounce and body, too. Fine, long hair tends to "pull down" your face.

If you have *small features* and a *slim body*, choose a short hairstyle like mine. Long hair or a very full head of hair will be too overpowering.

If you are *tall*, or have a *large face*, or are *big-boned*, your hairstyle should be full and at least shoulder length. A short hairstyle would be out of proportion with your shape.

If you have a *squarish face* (forehead or jawline), choose a style that falls softly around your face, not one that is pulled back or up.

If you have a *very high forehead*, try a style that includes bangs cut from the crown, rather than close to the hairline. Stay away from styles that pull hair off the forehead like a ponytail or a topknot.

If you have a *short neck*, pull hair away from your face into a chignon with tendrils to add length to your neck. If your *neck is long*, wear your hair long too; have it fall in curls.

Your lifestyle counts, too. *If you're very active*, a member of the swim team let's say, choose a style that's easy to care for—it should fall into place as it dries with gentle prodding from your fingers—not a formal style that requires a set.

Finding the right hairdresser goes hand in hand with finding the right cut. It's the hairdresser's experience and expertise that makes the cut work. Suga was able to see what a short style would do for me, even as I resisted. Some girls need length for a more feminine look; he said I didn't. He told me that short hair would enhance my eyes and give my cheeks more prominence as it balanced my round face.

It's always a question of getting all your features—and your hair is one of them—to work together. These decisions can be reached with the help of your hairdresser; we're not objective enough about ourselves to know what looks best. Your friends might agree with your ideas because they know it's what you want to hear, but a hairdresser can be impartial.

There are millions of beauty salons in small towns and large cities, but that doesn't mean they are all equally competent. A stylist might have earned his license, but that doesn't mean he or she will be creative. I don't think it's necessary or even practical for you to make a special trip to another city so that a famous hairstylist can work on you; I did it because of professional reasons. But it's no more in keeping with the private me than wearing false eyelashes offstage. No matter where you choose to get your hair cut, it has to be the best; this is the one area where you can't cut corners and expect it not to show. A bargain haircut is going to look like one, no matter what a fancy ad in a magazine or newspaper says. Unless you want to get scalped, be sure you're going to a reputable hair salon.

To find a good hairdresser where you live, there are many things you can do:

- Ask a girlfriend, whose new style you admire, to recommend her stylist.
- Look for the name of the stylist used in fashion or makeup articles in local magazines or newspapers, if you like his work.
- Ask your mother or your older sister to take you along on her next visit to the hairdresser and, while she's having her hair done, watch the different stylists at work.
- See if your favorite department store has a salon. To keep customers happy, it should be staffed with well-qualified technicians.

If you're on a budget, there are some ways of reducing the price of a good cut without harming its quality. Most salons charge for the cut, the shampoo, the conditioning, and the set or blow-out separately. You can save money by washing and conditioning your hair at home, right before your appointment. After your hair has been cut, it is wise to have it styled (set or blow-dried). If you pay careful attention now, you'll be able to style it yourself at home until it's time for a trim—ideally, every four to six weeks, depending on the length of your hair.

While you're at the hairdresser's . . . your stylist has other ways of improving on your hair.

55

PERMS

I have a body perm on my hair. This gives it more curl, versatility, and strength to withstand all the style changes I make during a one-hour show. When my hair is wet, it falls into tiny, tight curls. Depending on the style I want, I can change it to looser curls, a straight look, a partly curly and partly straight look, or a flipped-back curl, using either a curling iron, hot rollers, a blow dryer, or a combination. But it takes lots of practice to change the stubborn perm curls and a lot of extra conditioning that you're probably not used to.

If your hair is limp and needs body, or if it's reed straight and you'd like to try a curly, romantic look, think about getting a perm. But keep in mind that it has to grow out on its own and that takes a long time. (If you want to keep it, you'll need touch-ups, too.) Perms are also good for hair that's in between —neither really straight nor really curly. It will give it a defined look and a new shape. I even know a few guys who have had perms put in for just this reason!

STRAIGHTENING

If you have curly or frizzy hair and hate it, a straightening may be the answer for you. While a perm curls the hair, this opposite process relaxes the natural curl and makes hair lie flat and straight. Of the three techniques, this is the safest to do at home. There's no such thing as hair that's too straight, but if you're attempting a perm and don't really know what you're getting into, you *can* end up with hair that's too curly. Coloring your hair can be even more of a disaster! The directions on home-use preparations are easy enough; follow them faithfully. But for the best results, have a stylist do this the first time and watch carefully. He or she may be able to tell you how to manage on your own at home. Straightening usually has to be repeated once every four to six months, depending on how fast your hair grows and how much curl it has.

COLORING

Changing the color of your hair is a drastic step, one that I've never taken and don't recommend unless you're sure of what you want and are old enough to make the decision. I know that lots of girls would give almost anything to have blond hair, but not all of them are meant to have it. Changing the color of your hair might not be enough; to look natural you'd have to change your other coloring as well, and that's impossible. Your skin tone is an important factor to consider. Girls with olive or dark skin look best with dark hair; blond or red hair would look unnatural and make skin appear sallow. On the other side, girls with a pale, fair complexion can look freakish with black hair (the hardest color to switch to).

If you look closely at your hair, you'll see that it really isn't all red or all brown; there are subtle shadings in all hair. Unfortunately, most hair dyes don't take this into account. They strip your hair of all color and replace it with another, *one* other. Only a skilled colorist can know how to use these products to give dyed hair the natural tones that make hair so beautiful. I don't recommend you try any dyes at home that say *permanent* on the box. Temporary rinses that add color to light hair (they won't change brown or black hair) are okay, if you want to experiment. This color washes out in about six shampoos, and if it's a real disaster, you can shampoo six times in one night!

You can see how complicated coloring your hair is and why it's certainly not for everyone. If you'd like to add highlights to your hair, to make it shinier, you can rinse it with lemon juice if you're a blond, or with diluted vinegar if you have dark hair. Also try one of the new henna-enriched shampoos that add body and luster. This will give your hair more pizzazz, without the possibility of disastrous results.

Your hair needs extra-special care if you decide to have any of these processes done, or if you hair's been damaged by sun and wind to the point where it's dry and brittle. When looking for shampoos and conditioning products, always buy those that have been made especially for chemically treated hair. They have special ingredients that really nourish your hair from the outside in.

Hot rollers, hair dryers, curling irons, and hot combs, as well as natural heat from the sun, or a steam-heated room, all dry the delicate strands of hair. These can have damaging results on chemically treated hair. So don't use them more than two or three times a week and learn to maintain your hair properly at home. It's easy to do once you know the basics of hair care.

Hair Care at Home

I don't believe that you—or a friend—can cut your hair at home as well as a professional can. I'd never take a chance with that or with any other process that requires professional know-how. But there are many things you can do at home to improve your hair. Taking care of your hair is the best way to be sure it's full of color and sparkle. You have the time and the inclination that your stylist doesn't have (or would charge too much for!).

The three steps to healthy hair are *Shampoo–Rinse–Condition*. Shampooing cleans hair of dirt from pollution and oil that is secreted from the scalp. A special rinse continues the cleaning process, getting rid of any last traces of shampoo and gives hair a quick conditioning treatment. Conditioning is a way to give your hair a more intense kind of nourishing treatment, once or twice a month.

I wash my hair almost every day. I think it's important for you to wash yours when *you* need to. That's very individual. Girls with long hair, girls with oily hair, and girls who are very active might want and need to do it every night or morning. There's nothing wrong with this, as long as you use a mild shampoo formulated for your hair type: dry, oily, hard-to-manage, fine, dandruff prone. Dry hair is helped by a moisturizing shampoo. Oily hair can use an astringent-type shampoo, but not one with harsh detergents if you want to shampoo every night. Fine hair needs a protein shampoo for body. A very mild "baby" shampoo is good, too. If you have dandruff, commercial dandruff shampoos might be good, but if it's more than just a very light flaking, you'll need something stronger. Shampoos with tar and/or salicylic acid are effective, used every night for the first few days.

The rinse product you use should complement your shampoo. Try a treatment line for your hair; manufacturers design these component products to work together. A conditioning creme rinse is good for dry and hard-to-manage hair, but fine hair needs a lighter rinsing agent. Creams will coat fine hair and make it even more limp. Oily hair needs conditioning at the ends where oils may not always reach. One that contains real lemon is good, or rinse with fresh lemon juice squeezed before you shower; keep it in a handy plastic container.

I like to try new products all the time. Shampoos, like everything else, are always being improved. The older brands, formulated when shampooing was a once-a-week-only affair, have more detergents than the newer ones and can be damaging if used too often. But when you find a shampoo-and-rinse duo that really adds shine and bounce to your hair, stick with them. Here are some simple steps for getting the best shampoo.

SHAMPOO AND RINSE: YOU CAN'T HAVE ONE WITHOUT THE OTHER

1. Shampoo your hair in the shower to duplicate a professional shampoo, with your head leaning backward under the water, not forward as you would shampoo your hair in the sink. This prevents tangling and makes it easier to rinse.

2. Wet your hair thoroughly. This washes away superficial dirt and starts the cleaning process.

3. Pour the smallest amount of shampoo in the palm of your hand. Start with a quarter-sized dollop and increase, depending on the length of your hair.

4. Build the lather in your hands and work it through your hair, starting at your scalp and reaching all the way down to the ends.

5. Use finger*tips*, not nails, to massage your scalp and hair.

6. Rinse your hair under the shower until you can feel it squeak clean when you run your fingers along a strand.

7. Pour a dollop of your rinse product into the palm of your hand and work it through your hair to the ends. While shampoo is massaged into the scalp, this product is not. It's concentrated at the ends where you need the most conditioning.

8. Rinse your hair for two or three minutes until you're sure it is clean. Then rinse a few minutes longer.

9. When your shower's done, wrap your hair in a towel, turban style and let it soak up excess water. This is gentler than rubbing the hair and doesn't cause as much tangling. First "finger comb" your wet hair, then use a wide-toothed comb to detangle; a brush will stretch and break wet hair.

A *monthly conditioning* takes a little more time than the usual after-shampoo conditioning because you have to leave it on for half an hour, but it's worth the time, especially if you demand a lot from your hair, the way I do. A protein-enriched treatment pack penetrates the hair and beautifies it. If you have very dry hair, use it twice a month.

If you use electric appliances on your hair as I do, you should get a third kind of conditioner to apply before you blow dry or set it on hot rollers or under a hood dryer. I use ampules filled with a liquid conditioner that prepares the hair to handle the concentrated heat. You simply break them open and massage the liquid into your hair (not your scalp!) and go ahead with styling.

STYLING

Style it your way—not too many girls I know have the luxury of having their hair done for them. Unless I'm filming a movie

I love styling my own hair, but when I'm performing, it becomes work, and I need help from Gail Rowell, my hairdresser—and a very good friend.   PHOTOCRAFT

or a television show, I'm on my own, too. And when a professional does do my hair, it's more of a convenience than a luxury —I get some extra time to learn my lines!

I love doing my own hair because it's a challenge. By experimenting, I've learned a lot of different styles. I can work with a blow dryer (this loosens the tight perm curl) and then the curling iron (for touch-ups, small curls, and ringlets) or hot rollers (for a general curl). Or I can blow dry it twice—once for looseness and the second time around for the specific styling. The great thing about using the blow dryer is that you can keep going over your hair until you get it right.

When my family and I are performing in Las Vegas or on tour, I do three or four changes during the course of a single show. Each takes less than three minutes!—that's all the time I've got. Following are four examples of my quick-and-easy hairstyles.

Fortunately, I don't have to change my hair like this every day. It's neat to do it for the show because it enables me to play a lot of different parts and wear different fashion looks, but I'm glad that at home I can enjoy putting together one special look and not have to worry about quick changes!

Knowing how to work with your hair is vital, especially if you have a perm. If you can't use a blow dryer or hot rollers, you'll be stuck with a Shirley Temple look that can easily turn into Orphan Annie! But even if you don't have to worry about perm curls, it's fun to know how to achieve different looks—even long hair can be versatile if you know a little about hairstyling.

The easiest look is a haircut that dries into its style naturally, with only a little coaxing from your fingers to put the ends in place. But even these styles sometimes misbehave.

Your best ally is the *blow dryer*. Using this hand-held dryer and a brush or two, you can get your hair in shape. For straight hairstyles and for loosening permed hair, it's a must.

Aside from your blow dryer, you should have a round brush (a brush that has bristles all the way around) as well as a regular one, and four to eight plastic clips to hold the different sections of your hair. When using a blow dryer, you often feel as though you need three hands, one to hold the dryer, one to hold the brush, and the third to wrap sections of hair on the brush. The answer is to work in front of a mirrored counter so that you have somewhere to rest the dryer for the few seconds it takes to get the hair and the brush synchronized, without having to keep

The fun of short hair is learning to create new variations. I start with this casual look—no worries about its getting mussed when I'm having a lot of fun.

COURTESY OF HARRY LANGDON PHOTOGRAPHY

For a little extra flair, I like the swept-up look. I brush the hair to one side and accent with a barrette.

COURTESY OF HARRY LANGDON PHOTOGRAPHY

When I want to look pretty and extra feminine, I like the smooth style that comes from working with a round brush and a blow dryer.

COURTESY OF HARRY LANGDON PHOTOGRAPHY

For a very special occasion when the look is formal, I comb back my hair (using a light conditioner) and roll the ends at the nape of my neck.

COURTESY OF HARRY LANGDON PHOTOGRAPHY

65

turning the machine on and off. *Note:* If you're working in the bathroom, be sure to keep it away from any contact—however accidental—with water.

If you've just shampooed your hair and are still wearing the towel turban, take it off and run your fingers through your hair to untangle it. Use your wide-toothed comb to section it when it is almost dry. The drier your hair, the less heat you'll need from the blower and the less damaged it will get. (It can't be completely dry or it will be hard to style. If your hair has dried before you've had the chance to style it, use a plant mister to dampen it slightly.)

Now section your hair into four to eight areas, depending on how long and thick yours is: top, left and right sides, back. You can divide each side and the back into upper and lower sections. Pin each section with a clip so that you won't have to stop to part your hair again.

Starting on the right side, wrap the first section of hair around the brush. Be sure to get all the stray hairs so that you don't wind up with flyaways or frizzies. Have your blower set at a medium temperature—you don't want the damage the hottest one can cause. It'll hurt your wrist until you get used to it, but you're going to keep turning the brush, working it from the roots to the ends of your hair as the blower follows the motion. Keep the blow dryer moving, following the brush and perpendicular to it, so that the hot air isn't concentrated on one patch of hair for long. Keep the brush constantly rotating—it's easy with the round brush because you keep turning the handle; you don't have to stop to adjust it.

Always hold the dryer in the direction you want the hair to fall. If you're blowing it in a brushed-back style, like my first hairstyle, hold the dryer above your head and aim in downward with the nozzle perpendicular to the brush, not at your eye level.

When blow drying, the brush acts like a roller, giving the hair its shape; the heat of the dryer sets this shape. But some hair is very resistant, and that's why the action of gently pulling the hair up and out with the brush is necessary. You'll feel tension as your brush holds each section of hair taut. If you don't control your hair with the brush, it'll get "set" in the style *it* wants.

As each section dries and takes the basic shape, move on to the next section, working your way to the left side. Do the upper section and then the front. (You may have to dampen the front if it took you awhile to get the hang of the dryer.) Always make sure that the ends have been wrapped around the brush correctly, even if it means putting down the blower and replacing that section of hair on the brush.

Once you have the base of your style, you're ready to go over crucial areas to perfect the look. Concentrate on the strays around the hairline; they have to be moving in the same direction as the main body of hair. See which sections look a little out of whack or stand out from the rest. You may want to mist the ends lightly and redo them. Don't neglect the back or the sides to concentrate on the front; all the sections need equal attention because they must work together. I like to use the regular brush to smooth the sections. With the first brush, you held the hair over the brush. Now you'll smooth the brush over the hair.

If my hair is acting up, if the direction doesn't look right, now is the time to pop in a few large size hot rollers to give it more definition. (If I want smaller curls, on top or the sides, I use smaller rollers.) You may need the rollers for only a second, and only in certain sections. Take them out quickly and brush all the hair together. You may want to give it another turn with the dryer. When you're satisfied with the way it looks, finish your styling with a light touch of hair spray to hold it. But I never put the spray directly on my hair—that gives a stiff, phony look and only reaches the top hairs. Instead, spray it on your regular hair brush and brush it through in the direction you've styled your hair.

Other styles call for other appliances. Blow dryers are great as a first step in styling, or for achieving straight or slightly curved looks. For curlier styles, you'll need to use hot rollers and/or a curling iron. You can work with regular rollers and set your hair wet, but these take forever to work, unless you're willing to sit under the dryer for an hour—and hood dryers are expensive! I don't have the time to waste setting my hair on rollers; I have too many fun things to do instead. And you certainly shouldn't wear them outside as I see many girls do. There's no quicker way to scare off a guy than to walk around with rollers in your hair, even if you try to hide them with a scarf. With these convenient appliances, all you need is ten minutes and you've got a great set.

Hot rollers. I set my blow-dried hair on these to give a curly look—all over or only in front or back. Most sets come with a variety of rollers: small ones for tight curls, medium ones for full curls, and large ones for gentle curves.

Heat them according to the directions and while you're waiting, have end papers and a comb for sectioning ready. Section your hair as you did for blow drying. If your hair is very long or thick, divide each section in two. Before you roll each section, take an end paper and wrap it around the ends. This protects them from drying out and keeps any strays from escaping.

For a soft curl, roll the hair around the hot rollers straight up from the ends. But if you want the curl tighter, brush the hair straight out so that it's parallel to your shoulder, and you can roll it practically to the roots.

Leave the rollers in for about ten minutes. In that time, the heat will dissipate. You can leave them in a little longer while you put on your makeup without worrying about drying out the hair. You won't get any extra heat, but these extra minutes will help strengthen the set. When you take out the rollers and are brushing the hair into place, spray the brush with hair spray to help hold the set.

Curling iron. This is a handy appliance to have if you need a quick touch-up. Although it's not too good to use every day, it can add quick curls after blow drying or natural drying, when time is of the essence. Each section of hair is rolled on the iron, one at a time, held in the clip for a few seconds, and released. Because the hot metal curler can damage hair, be sure the one you buy is Teflon coated. I don't recommend a curling iron for very long hair because it can handle only a small amount of hair at a time.

Note: If you're going to use hot rollers or a curling iron on your hair and if you don't have a perm that needs loosening beforehand, let your hair dry naturally first as often as you can. This cuts down on the amount of artificial drying and setting. Hair must be dry when using either of these two setting helpers.

Long hair likes variety, too. My pictures show you how easy it is to change from one short style to another, but as I told you, not everyone looks neat with short hair. Girls with long hair can do more than wear it loose and long. Ponytails can be nice, but there's so much more you can do.

*Swiss braids:*Make two braids, one on each side of your head and wrap them across your crown. Fasten with pins or fancy hair combs.

Topknot: Bend over and back brush your hair into a ponytail at the top of your head and secure with a fabric-covered rubberband. Now twist the tail into a roll around the band, tucking the ends underneath and fasten with bobby pins. Use more pins to fasten a small spray of paper or silk flowers on either side of the "knot."

French chignon: Brush all your hair into a ponytail, but instead of securing it, roll it under, tucking in the ends. Secure with pins and a fan-shaped comb.

Nape roll: Part your hair down the center, from front to back and twist each half into a roll, one at a time, at the nape of your neck. They should meet in the back. Gently pull a few strands of hair loose at the hairline on each side and set in two small hot rollers for romantic tendrils.

Spray of curls: Make a ponytail at the top of your head and set the ends in lots of small hot rollers. When you take them out, you'll have a cascade of curls.

A Guide to Buying Hair Setting and Styling Helpers

There's a wide variety of appliances to choose from, at all different prices. And a lot of the items aren't at all necessary. If I had to choose two, I'd pick a good blow dryer and a set of hot rollers. (The curling iron isn't really that necessary unless you have to make instant repairs backstage, like I do, and don't have time to wait for rollers to heat up.)

Blow dryers. There are probably more of these in different shapes and sizes than there are Osmonds! Some are extra large and extra powerful; others are small and lightweight. What you should look for: 1) power. That's measured by the number of watts. If possible, get a dryer that has settings for 800–1000 watts; that's strong enough. 2) two or more different settings that let you regulate the heat and power. One setting alone can give you too much at once and can dry out your hair. What you don't need are a lot of attachments. Some dryers have nozzles that concentrate the air on one section and can easily dry hair out. Detangling comb attachments don't really do all that much; you can save this expense too. But do get a round brush to use with the dryer.

Hot rollers. I use a lot of small hot rollers—so many, in fact, that I had to get two sets to have enough. I wish someone would make sets that have only small, medium, or large rollers. But until they do, we'll have to get by with the mixed type. Hot rollers with mist settings are gentle on your hair. But if you use hot rollers only three times a week, with end papers, and always use a hair rinse or conditioner on delicate hair, any type is good, and the more rollers in each size the better, if you want to vary your hairstyles.

Curling iron. It bears repeating: If you think you'd like to get one, make sure it is coated with a nonstick surface like Teflon to protect your hair. Before applying it to your hair, always test it with an end paper. If the paper burns, the iron's too hot. Put it on a lower setting, or if it doesn't have one, let it cool and test again before you start.

HAIR DO'S . . .

Relax; stress causes premature gray hair!

Eat a wholesome diet for healthy, shiny hair.

Brush as little as possible if you have oily hair; brushing makes it oilier.

In summer: Condition frequently to make up for damage by chlorine in pools, salt in the ocean, excess perspiration.

AND DON'TS

Don't worry if you notice your hair falling out; 100 hairs a day is normal.

Don't brush 100 strokes every day; that's too much for hair to take.

Don't massage your scalp; that makes it oilier, too.

Don't leave your scalp unprotected if you part your hair; use sunscreen or wear a pretty summer hat.

70

HAIR DO'S . . .   AND DON'TS

In winter: Protect your hair with hats and hoods.

Don't let hair fly loose in the wind; wear it in a ponytail or chignon if it's long, but not every day as this too can damage hair.

BEAUTY TOOLS FOR HAIR CARE

- Flat-backed brush
- Round-shaped brush for styling
- Wide-toothed comb
- Bobby pins to secure hair and hair accessories
- Fashion hair combs and flowers
- Plant mister
- Shampoo–rinse–conditioner treatment line
- Pump bottle, nonaerosol hair spray
- Blow dryer
- Hot rollers
- Curling iron (optional)

Special note: Your hair helpers—brushes, combs, and hair accessories—should be washed as often as you wash your hair, either in a bowl of soapy water or shampoo. And remember to rinse your combs and brushes as thoroughly as you do your own hair.

5.

The Beauty Part:
A Little Extra Glamor

JUST AS LITTLE makeup touches form your special look, little extra touches improve it. There are things a girl does, which no one sees, that can make her look extra special. And then there are others that are very noticeable. I've put them together in this chapter because they can give a girl a lot of style and a little extra glamor that make her look good and feel good, too. Feeling good about yourself is especially important; if you're confident and proud of yourself, the people you meet will be, too.

When It's Time to De-Fuzz

You may not think that shaving is especially glamorous, but there's nothing great about unwanted hair. No one's really going to compliment you on your shaving, but people do notice when you don't! Lots of young girls are afraid their body hair will get thicker or darker once they start shaving—but that's not true. The real question is exactly when you should begin. There's really no one age—girls mature at different times. It's a personal question you and your mother should decide together. Mothers are really great ladies—they know so much more than we do (though we may not always agree), because they've been through it all before.

I think that you should start considering shaving when you begin to notice that the light fuzz has turned to darker hair. As you become more concerned with your appearance, you'll want to improve the way you look—and this is definitely one way of becoming more feminine and attractive.

There are five ways to de-fuzz, and they vary in terms of cost and how often they must be repeated. There's one thing they do have in common: They all work!

1) *Waxing*. This process really shouldn't be done at home, but at a salon that specializes in it. Warm wax is applied to your legs, allowed to harden, and is then pulled off. Ouch! It doesn't just tickle; it can sting. Why do women still have it done, even though it can cost up to twenty dollars? Because it pulls the hair out at the roots and prevents stubble for up to a month. It's also quick and effective on upper-lip hair.

2) *Depilatory*. This foam or lotion is applied at home and it dissolves hair in about twenty minutes. It's easy to do yourself and each application costs only a couple of dollars. But some girls' skin gets an allergic reaction from the chemicals in the product. You'll have to do a patch test on your wrist the day before to see if you are allergic to it, especially if you plan to use it on your face. Follow package directions carefully. The only other drawback is that the depilatories all smell a little . . . funny.

3) *Bleaching*. There are inexpensive creams available that lighten the hair in a few minutes. But if your hair is thick, lightening it won't be enough. Many girls bleach facial hair above the upper lip, but the hair is still there. If your eyebrows are very dark, you can lighten them with a hair bleach just for that but be careful how long you leave it on or you'll wind up looking like Santa Claus. This technique is only for the advanced beauty student!

4) *Electrolysis*. This is a very expensive procedure, performed by a trained professional, which destroys individual hair shafts and permanently removes the hair. It can be painful because it is done by inserting a small needle into each follicle (or hair shaft) and passing a small electric charge through it. It's also very time consuming because only a little hair can be removed during each session. And like I said, it's painful. But if you have bothersome facial hair that could be worsening clogged pores or is very unsightly, you might want to talk over this alternative with your parents.

5) *Shaving*. This is the quickest, easiest, and least expensive way to remove hair, especially on your legs and underarms. Some girls like to use electric shavers to avoid nicks and cuts, but they don't give you as smooth a shave as a regular razor.

There are special "ladies' razors" designed to reach all the

73

angles of a girl's body (particularly around the knees). And they come in pretty colors so that you never have to bother your father by mistakenly using his! You'll also need a softening agent for a smooth shave. Shaving cream gives a nice lather, but using a body lotion is a good idea, too. It doesn't hide the hairs like a thick lather does, and it gives you a very smooth finish. In a pinch, you can lather with a bar of soap, but never use a slick oil or greasy liquid that can clog the razor and your pores, and never shave dry.

The best place to shave is in the bathroom. Sit on the edge of the tub with your legs inside. The faucet makes it easy to rinse the razor (after every stroke) and your legs, to see where touch-ups are needed. Place a towel on the rim before you sit down for secure positioning.

HOW TO SHAVE:

1. After rinsing your legs (or underarms) with soap and warm water to soften hairs, apply your shaving lotion or lather.

2. Use long, smooth strokes to remove hair. Shaving against the direction in which the hair grows will give you a closer shave. Go slowly to avoid nicks. If the hair is coming off only with a struggle, it's time to change blades or cartridges.

3. Rinse the razor after each stroke. And apply extra lotion as you need it.

4. If you're shaving under your arms, you'll see that the hairs grow in all different directions. Change angles for the cleanest shave.

5. When you think you're finished, rinse all the extra lotion off your skin and check your work. Natural light will tell how well you've done, so dry off and check in front of your bedroom window if you can. Any strays? Put on a little more lotion and shave these spots.

6. If you've used body lotion while shaving, you should have a silky soft skin. If you didn't or if your skin is very dry, apply it now.

7. Don't forget to clean your razor thoroughly before putting it away, and make sure all the shaved hairs are rinsed away, too.

Special tips for a better shave:
1. If you should nick yourself, let cold water run over the cut

to stop the bleeding and apply a little antibacterial salve when dry.

2. If you notice little red bumps after shaving (a common irritation) apply a little alcohol to the area. Before your next shave, first wash with antibacterial soap, and soak your razor in alcohol to get rid of any bacteria. Change blades frequently, too.

3. For a more comfortable shave, buy a razor that uses cartridges. Don't handle double-edged razor blades if you don't have to.

4. Don't use deodorant after shaving your underarms unless it's a brand that says it's okay. It can sting as it gets inside open pores. Use baby powder instead.

5. Shave in the evening, if you can, to let skin recuperate overnight.

6. You won't have to shave every day, and hair won't grow back heavier once you start. But shaving is one of the beauty steps that has to be repeated. How often depends on how fast your hair grows back. You should check often—some girls need to shave only once every week or two; others twice a week.

7. If you have any embarrasing hair growth, don't be afraid to talk about it with your mother or even your school nurse. Some girls have lots of unwanted hair; others have less or even none. It all depends on your body's glandular system and has nothing to do with you as a person.

SOME MORE HAIR-RAISING NEWS

Excess facial hair is a problem many girls have (and I've given you some ideas about how to get rid of it), but the facial hair that gets the most attention is that of your eyebrows. I wonder if the person who invented tweezers knew what calamity he was creating! I've seen girls who have thinned their brows so much that they look like pencil marks and other girls who haven't done enough tweezing.

Everyone's brows are as different as their fingerprints, but there's one easy rule to follow for beginning to reshape your eyebrows: They should be parallel to the natural curve of the upper eyelid's lashline. Of course, there are girls whose brows are perfect and they shouldn't touch them, but for the rest of us who need a little help . . . slant-edged tweezers to the rescue! Be careful that first time you use them because you can lose your natural curve if you pluck without thinking.

Here are some steps to follow, whether you need a little tweezing or a lot:

1. Think of your eyebrows as frames for your eyes. You want a frame that enhances them, not one that is so overpowering it takes away the attention they get.

2. On the other hand, no one wants to look scalped! Always use the natural curve of your brow as your guide.

3. Start by cleaning brows and tweezers with cotton saturated in alcohol or astringent. The brow should start right above the inner corner of the eye. Tweeze any hairs that are growing toward the nose or on the bridge of the nose. Brows shouldn't be too thin, but if yours are very low, thin the whole brow from underneath. Don't lower it from the top. To know how high they should be, feel your brow bone with a fingertip; they should start at the top of the bone.

4. Stray hairs growing above the natural curve can be tweezed, too. Done properly, this won't lower the brow, just make it neater.

5. Don't exaggerate the arch. The brow shouldn't end in a dramatic point but taper off gradually. Again, remember to follow your own natural brows.

6. After tweezing, cleanse the area again with astringent or alcohol, to prevent redness. Don't apply any makeup (this can clog the pores). Tweezing should be done at night, like shaving, to give any redness a chance to clear.

7. Check for stray hairs every night; makeup, like eye shadow, will cling to them and make them more noticeable.

Special note: If your eyebrow hairs are extra long, but still within the curve of the brow, you can clip them with small manicure-sized scissors.

Where not to pluck:

• Visible hairs inside your nostrils—this could cause an infection. Clip, don't tweeze, only the hairs that show (you need the others for filtering the air you breathe). Use blunt-edged scissors.

• Hair growing from a beauty mark or mole. Clip with blunt-edged scissors.

• Hair above your upper lip: This area's too painful and sensitive to tweeze. Use one of the other hair de-fuzzing techniques.

The Beauty of Your Hands

It's often the little things that tell the most about our personality. When a girl has a beautifully manicured set of nails—she doesn't even have to be wearing polish—it says that she cares about herself. And what's more, caring can be fun. An hour of special attention you give to yourself can boost your spirits and give you hands you'll want to show off. Here's how to give them a real "cure":

1. Start every manicure by removing old polish (if you wear it). *Nail polish remover* used to have a very unpleasant odor but now you can buy gentler formulations with herbal scents that condition as they remove color.

2. The second step is *shaping* your nails. Use an *emery board* to taper your nails to a reasonable length, about a ¼ inch long (measured from the point the nail extends past the fingerpad). You might want them shorter if you're very active—long nails break more easily when your hands are involved in the action or if you type or play piano or guitar. Round the corners, but don't file the sides of the nails because this can weaken them. And always file in one direction only, not in a back-and-forth motion.

3. For a professional feel and look, *soak* your fingertips in a warm, soapy basin of water for three minutes. If you want to *soften* and *nourish* nails and fingers, add some *baby oil* to the water.

4. Too much is made of cuticles. I've never had to cut or trim mine—if you don't bother them, they won't bother you! Cuticle scissors are one of the first things you should take out of your manicure kit. (Tie a ribbon around them and slip them into your mother's sewing box.) Cutting cuticles is an unnecessary hazard. If yours are that obvious, after soaking gently *push them back* with a *cotton-tipped orangewood stick*. Cuticle cream will soften them, too, and nourish the nail, but it's the last thing you should put on your list (if you use it, now is the time).

5. Healthy nails have a natural shine. You can add luster

to your nails by *buffing* them. Using a *cream* or *paste* with a natural-hide *buffing brush* will make them pretty without polish (and nails can use a rest from that every now and then). Buffing helps improve circulation, too—that's important if your fingers are the first to get cold in cool weather. The buffer brush gently works the cream or paste into the nail. Brush in one direction, just as you filed.

6. Weak nails need a little *strengthening*. Ladies used to drink gelatin beverages, but that's an old idea. Today, nail products like *protein cream* and *clear fortified polish* work much faster. Choose the cream if you don't wear polish. If you prefer tinted polish, choose a brand that is formulated with strengtheners. And remember to keep an eye toward nutrition. Healthy nails require calcium, found in dairy products like milk and yogurt.

7. Nail *polish* is where the glamor really shows. But I think that you have to approach this step carefully. I don't think that younger girls look right with darker polish on their fingers—it's really out of place. I didn't start until I was dating, and my first polish was a clear one that added shine and protection. Soft pinks and beiges are good colors, too. Wait until you can carry a deeper red—about the time you're old enough to wear that shade of lipstick.

Coordinating lipstick and nail color is as important as choosing the right lipstick, blush, and shadow. And if you wear lip gloss, you should know that there are new nail polishes that give the same kind of sheer look to nails—tint and shine without opaque color.

Follow these steps to a better nail polish application:
- Start by applying a *clear base coat* to protect nails from staining by colored polishes and to give that polish a smooth surface. Use three strokes: the first down the center of the nail, the second on the right side, the third on the left. The strokes should blend into each other.
- Allow the base to dry and then apply the first coat of color, using the same three-stroke application.
- Allow this coat to dry and repeat it.
- When dry, re-apply the clear base coat or, if you can afford another product, a *clear sealer*. Let it dry.
- Rotate your wrists to get the air around your nails circulating;

this will help them dry faster. Be sure to allow them to dry thoroughly before using your hands, or you'll smudge the polish and have to begin again.

Special note: If you chip a nail and have time to remove the old polish before applying a new coat, be sure that you rinse the nail after you've used the remover to get rid of any last traces that could blend with new polish and change its texture.

R & R: REPLACEMENT AND REPAIR

With ten of them to worry about, sooner or later you're going to break a fingernail. Whether or not you catch it as the tip is about to come off, you can mend your nail or put on a replacement without disturbing any of the others or ruining your manicure. One of these surefire emergency kits is all you need.

1. *The repair kit*—to seal a torn edge or even reattach one that's come off. These contain a liquid and fabric that work together to patch over the rip. You can slowly file off the repaired part as the nail grows.

2. *The replacement tips*—to add length to the broken nail. This kit comes with crescent-shaped tips that you glue onto the edge of the nail you want to extend. You can do all of them or just the one(s) that needs it in an emergency. They grow out as your nail does.

3. *The replacement nails*—the temporary solution. Full nails are applied directly over your own and are worn for up to two days at a time. The only drawback is that they may not fit the exact contour of your nail.

4. *The brush-on nails*—to build over your own. With a mix of powder and liquid, you brush on nail-like material over your own and onto a form to extend them. You file the nail edge as desired. The advantage here is that you build the nail along your natural contours.

To look as natural as possible, you should use nail polish afterward. It hides any line that might show where your nail meets the impersonator. For most girls, wearing false nails is impractical for every day. We are too busy to worry about whether or not false nails are still on. But there are times when we'd like a perfect set and a little R & R can fix any damage done by our active lives.

Special care for the active girl:
- Keep nails trim; they won't break as often if they're short.
- After the soak (step 3 of manicure), use a pumice stone to gently remove any dead skin around a callus.
- If a nail is damaged (you're playing tennis and your hand is hit by the ball, for instance) and you see it turning black, don't panic. This darkness is just a little bleeding under the nail. Be patient; it'll grow out. If it's really unattractive and you have to look your best, use a neutral, flesh-toned polish on all your nails, and in the future be careful.
- If you wear polish, keep the bottle with you at all times for emergency touch-ups.

Your Feet Need Some Attention, Too

It's very important to care for your feet; they control the health of your body because they hold your weight. You feel better when your feet look their best, especially in the summertime. Because I have to dance so much during our weekly rehearsals and the shows, I depend on my feet and treat them to a pedicure once a week. Probably, though, once every two weeks is enough (the manicure is a weekly must for every girl).

Follow the steps for the manicure, but because feet do so much more hard labor, here are a few bonuses:

1. If you can, invest in a bath-like mini-whirlpool. They're great, especially if you stand or walk a lot during the day. If not, you can rest your feet in a basin of warm water mixed with Epsom salts for ten minutes.

2. After the soak, use a *pumice stone* to gently remove dead skin on the sole or heel of each foot. I put some lemon juice on my heels (and knees and elbows) to cleanse them, too.

3. Use a toenail clipper rather than a file to trim nails straight across for the sleekest look. This is a must in summer when strappy sandals put your feet on display.

4. Use a nailbrush across the toes as well as under the nails; this removes dead cuticles easily.

5. Treat your feet to a heavy-duty lotion or cream to pamper them. For a special overnight treatment, slather on the cream and, without rubbing off the excess, slip into a pair of white cotton socks. This will "bathe" your feet without getting your sheets greasy.

6. Take ten minutes in the evening, before you go to sleep, to prop your feet under two fat pillows so that they are raised above your heart. This improves circulation, gives them a much deserved rest, and prevents varicose veins, too.

7. If you're going to polish your toenails, consider buying a toe separator from your cosmetics store. It's made out of cork or rubber and has four prongs that slip between toes to keep them from touching as the polish dries. And check your toes as often as you check your nails for touch-ups.

The Romance of Perfume

Fragrance is a very special part of my good grooming. For me, it always adds a little extra femininity especially when I'm working with my brothers. Developing my own perfume, called *Marie*, was one of my most terrific beauty experiences. I sampled more than fifty combinations of different notes (or scents) until I picked the final formula of jasmine, rose, and hyacinth—a floral perfume, yet a light one. We had it made into a cologne instead of a heavy, all oil-based perfume because light scents are more refreshing on young girls. (I think that a heavy concentration of fragrance can nearly sicken those you are with!) I love the fresh, light scent—just a hint of fragrance and smells as though you were just sprayed with a floral powder. It's great.

Putting on the touch of fragrance can be as simple as squeezing a lemon and using the juice as a rinse for your hair—a fresh scent that's delicious, too. And there are many lemon-scented colognes you can buy—the best introduction to this special world.

It's nice to be able to splash yourself with *cologne* or *eau de toilette* after a bath or shower and on hot, humid days. It can really cool you off. But when you use *perfume*, you should use it sparingly, just a drop or two on your pulse points: behind your knees, in the crook of your arms, beneath your neck, at your wrists. But these are only three of the many forms of fragrance. To feel totally wrapped in your favorite scent, you should also have dusting powder or shaker talc, bath oil, and a solid sachet in a small compact for on-the-go perfuming.

There's no getting away from expensive perfume prices, but you can choose any of the other concentrations—that's another reason *Marie* was made into a cologne. It's easier on your allowance! Most perfume scents are available in cologne form. The biggest problem you'll have is choosing one of the hundreds offered.

When you're sampling colognes, try only two at any one time because your nose can easily get confused. Use a tester to spray it on your wrist. Don't take the bottle's word for the scent—what you're inhaling are only the top notes, the first to be released. After you've worn the scent for a few minutes, the next set of notes, the middle notes, become more apparent—the fragrance has started to mix with your skin's chemistry. After twenty minutes, the base notes emerge—this is what the scent will be like until you refresh it, so you should really like these more than the top notes.

When you find a cologne you're sure of, buy a small bottle first. Tastes change and you might not like it as much next month. But be sure to use it frequently—perfumes and colognes are high in alcohol content and can evaporate quickly. You don't want to wait to use them and then find the bottle empty!

Here are some special tips for wearing cologne (or perfume):

- Always apply fragrance before getting dressed (it can cling to clothes) and before you put on any jewelry (it can ruin pearls and many other baubles).
- Cologne is great for girls with oily skin. But girls with dry skin can find it irritating or that it doesn't last long. Try a perfume oil (not as expensive as perfume because it's a single extract) like jasmine, tuberose, lavender, or violet.
- Keep your fragrances out of direct light and away from extreme heat. A cool, dark shelf is the best place to prevent evaporation.
- Layer your fragrance products to surround yourself with perfume. After soaking in the tub with bath oil, dust yourself with

powder, and splash on cologne or eau de toilette—all in the same scent.

The Sparkle of Jewelry

There's nothing like wearing jewelry to make me feel glamorous and grown-up. But I don't like gaudy jewelry or wearing too much at once. I have been collecting earrings since I was a little girl, and word has spread because I always receive new pairs as holiday gifts. But there's something very special about the earrings and the other small pieces that I have bought for myself. If you've ever saved up your allowance to buy something you've wanted for a long time, you'll know what I mean. Unlike makeup and even clothes, jewelry is something you'll have forever and, even better, it never goes out of style.

Real gold jewelry is nice to have, even if it's only a thin gold chain with a charm hanging from it. A pinkie ring with a tiny, semi-precious stone chip is pretty, too, and can cost less than twenty dollars. The most exciting gold jewelry I've had was my first set of pierced earrings. They were small, round studs, like two miniature Christmas balls—the first night I was able to wear them was when the jacket photo for "Winning Combination" was being taken and I was so proud of them I made sure you could see them from every angle!

If you're going to wear earrings, I think that piercing your ears is a good thing to do. It's protection against losing one earring that might not be easily replaceable, especially if you're lucky enough to wear your grandmother's antique studs. I carefully studied the procedure before my ears were pierced so that I would know exactly what was happening. The ear is actually pierced through to make a tiny hole. It's really quite painless; the ear is frozen or anesthetized so you don't feel anything. You can ask your doctor to do it or go to a shop that specializes in it (usually the piercing and your first set of earrings can be had for the same price as the earrings alone), but just to be on the safe side, check with your local Better Business Bureau before you decide on a jewelry shop.

I gave my ears special attention for three weeks (although many people will tell you that ten to fourteen days is enough). I smelled like a doctor's office, but I don't believe that you should take any chances with your health. Three to six times a day, I cleansed the earlobes with a cotton swab dipped in strong alcohol. Before bed, I did this with hydrogen peroxide and then applied a good antibacterial salve like Neosporin, turning the stud in each ear to make sure the area was well covered. After three weeks, when I was able to wear any earrings, I always made sure to wipe them and my ears with the alcohol before and after putting them in.

Taking care of your jewelry, whether it's real or the fun costume kind, putting it back in its case after you've worn it, keeping each piece clean, insures that it will last longer and look its brightest. A jeweler uses special cleaning solution along with an old toothbrush to keep gold sparkling. You might want to get a bottle of it if you have a lot of jewelry and wear it frequently. If not, the jeweler can clean your pieces when you go to select a new chain or pin.

If you don't have a special jewelry box, you can make one by lining a small gift box with velvet—this soft fabric keeps jewelry from scratching against hard surfaces. You can section it off with strips of stiff cardboard also covered with the fabric—this will keep the different pieces of jewelry from scratching each other.

Like makeup, the jewelry you choose to wear should be appropriate to the situation. Heavy makeup and your best necklace will look all wrong on a hike; stud earrings, if your ears are pierced, and maybe a class ring, if you wear it all the time, are more than enough. Jewelry is a fashion accessory—it can complement or kill an outfit. Remember—it's not how much you have, but how you wear it that really spells glamor.

BEAUTY BASICS FOR A LITTLE EXTRA GLAMOR

- *To de-fuzz:*
  Cartridge razor blade and shaving cream OR electric
    razor OR depilatory
  Body lotion

- *For eyebrow shaping:*
  Eyebrow brush (from chapter 3)
  Tweezers, slant-edged
  Alcohol/astringent

- *For manicure and pedicure:*
  Emery board
  Toenail clippers
  Cuticle cream
  Baby oil
  Orangewood stick and cotton
  Buffing kit with cream or paste and a buffer
  Nail cream for strengthening
  Polish: clear for base and top coats, tinted to match
    lipsticks
  Polish remover
  Replacement nails
  Pumice stone
  Nail brush, natural bristle
  Hand cream or lotion (good for feet, too)

- *Your fragrance wardrobe* (any combination of the
    following):
  Perfume
  Cologne
  Eau de toilette
  Bath oil
  Bath/dusting powder
  Cream sachet

- *Your jewelry wardrobe* (should start with a gift from your
    parents—they'll know when you're ready):
  Narrow gold or gold-finished chain with a small charm
  Pair of small gold earrings
  Thin gold bracelet
  Strand of baby pearls

6.
Memo from Marie: A Checklist for Beauty

IN EVERY CHAPTER of the Beauty and Health parts, there is a list of the essential items and tools you'll need to look your best. Many of the extra beauty helpers are duplicates. These products do a lot of different jobs equally well.

Petroleum jelly lubricates lashes and acts like mascara by making them shiny. It also lubricates your lips and takes the place of gloss, if you aren't wearing it yet. It's also great for controlling your eyebrows and even removing makeup around the delicate eye area—you don't have to rub or pull this tender skin, just slide it on and off with tissue. (Tissues, cotton balls, and swabs are helpful, too, in applying and removing creams, makeup, and lotions, as well as nail polish.)

Baby products are still good even though you're certainly not a baby anymore. *Baby talc* is great for lengthening lashes (when used with mascara), applying a silky finish after your bath, controlling a shiny nose and even giving your hair a dry shampoo when you don't have time for the real thing. Sprinkle it liberally on your hair, allow it to soak up dirt and oil for two minutes and brush it out.

Baby oil, lightly applied, gives dry skin a good base for makeup and lubricates at night, too, after cleansing (a vacation from your moisturizer). It's great for dry skin all over. Squeeze a liberal amount into your next tub and come out feeling silky. You can use it to remove makeup and condition lips, too.

Baby cream can also do these jobs (except soften bath water). It's great for soothing chafed skin and softening feet, elbows, and knees overnight.

By using one of these products for two or three different jobs, you shorten the list of beauty helpers and the amount you'll have to spend. You'll probably find most of these in your home already.

When you're buying beauty basics, it's important to get the best values possible—the most advertised ones aren't always the best. There are some stores that will have what you need at much lower prices than department and specialty stores. "Health and Beauty Aid" stores offer the same brands as most expensive cosmetic counters, but at discount prices even lower than discount drugstores (the difference is that they don't sell prescription items) and the five-and-dime. Chain stores price beauty aids at lower costs than more exclusive (translation: expensive) stores. It's still nice to shop at luxury department stores, but not when you're on a budget (and every dollar counts). It's really worth the trouble of going out of your way to reach a discount center, especially if you can stock up at one time.

Take a look at the different lists I've given so far and make up your own specialized one. Be sure to check with your mom to see what she might already have and what brands she thinks are best. Check the free newspapers that are often left in your mailbox (the kind that has television listings and plenty of ads) to see which stores advertise the best sale prices. And before you buy, check the difference in price on products that aren't on "special." They may be higher at the store with the most terrific values, to keep the owner's profits high. In that case, it's worth it to buy the sale items here and get the rest at another store.

I like to keep a journal, and in it I put all the important things I want to remember. Yours could include the addresses of the best Health and Beauty Aid stores, those with the best selection and the best prices. Try these suggestions too:

- Once you've found a product that works for you, buy the largest size you can. Ounce per ounce, it's usually less expensive. Though it's a bigger expense at the beginning, one 16-ounce bottle of astringent will cost less, in the long run, than two separate purchases of 8-ounce bottles.
- Keep a running list of the products you use and see how long each lasts; maybe a new brand will be more economical. This list should also note when you're going to need to visit the discount store again.
- Some beauty tools can be the store's own brand, saving you even more. These are items like cotton balls and swabs, facial tissues, alcohol, and all-purpose body lotion.
- Beauty suppliers that sell to salons often offer private custom-

ers the same discounts. Check in your Yellow Pages for one near you.

• If your beauty list is very long, divide it into four or eight mini-lists; you'll have no problem filling one each week. It's easier than trying to afford everything at once.

7.

The Health Part:
Food or Your Figure—
What's More Important?

ONE OF THE times my brother Jay and I went on a double date was a Valentine's Day. All four of us thought it would be fun to write down four things we were most grateful for. I was busy listing funny things, but Jay and our dates had each chosen good health as one blessing. That started me thinking. I've often heard that if you don't have your health, you really don't have anything. That little game we played made me realize just how true that saying is.

If you're not physically fit, you can't enjoy anything—you're run down and you feel miserable. As if that weren't enough, your skin, your hair, your nails are affected, too. You don't look any healthier on the outside than you are on the inside. I went through a time when I wasn't eating properly, and I suffered with frequent colds because of it. That's why eating the right foods from these different food groups is very important:

(1) *Lean meats*, like veal and lamb; *poultry*, like chicken and turkey; *eggs*; *fish* and *shellfish* give you lots of protein. I don't think that you need as much red meat as you do seafood and poultry because steak, pork and some lamb contain plenty of animal fat (not so nutritious) between meat fibers as well as around them. Chicken and fish fillets are much better (so is liver).

Beans, like lentils; and *nuts* have lots of protein too. They are also high in calories, but if it's a choice between a snack of candy or peanuts, choose the nuts.

(2) *Milk* and other *dairy products* provide you with minerals as well as protein, carbohydrates, and fat. Lean cheeses, cottage cheese, and yogurt are delicious and low in calories. Ice cream, butter, and cream cheeses are tasty too, but much higher in calories because they contain so much fat.

(3) *Whole wheat products*, like breads and cereals; *pasta* and

Shopping . . .

. . . and cooking can be fun!

other *starches* give you carbohydrates, minerals, and vitamins. Refined foods like store-bought white bread and bleached flour give you calories but not much else. My mother mills her own wheat and bakes fresh bread, but that's not something most city parents can do. Try whole wheat breads from the supermarket and whole grain cereals that you cook instead of those that list sugar as a main ingredient.

(4) *Fruits* and *vegetables* have natural sugar for taste and carbohydrates for energy. There's little fat and protein here but plenty of vitamins and minerals.

If it sounds like I'm concerned about eating well, it's because I'm thinking of my body and also of the children I hope to have someday. Our health controls theirs, and even if you're just beginning to think about the future, it takes a lot of planning— you should be in good shape three to five years before you even think of having a family. I don't want to scare you, but you should be aware of how important your body is. That's why I don't believe in smoking or drinking stimulants of any kind (that includes beer, wine, tea, and coffee). Aside from not having any nutritional value, they're just plain bad for you. Alcohol attacks your vital organs—your liver, your heart, and your nervous system; smoking harms your lungs and your heart. I don't think that any temporary high or feeling of superiority happens to be worth that. Your body is an intricate machine, and it has to be cared for in a special way to keep running.

Eating and drinking the wrong foods may show on the outside as well as on the inside. Junk foods, like greasy fries and burgers, deep-fried fish and chicken, not only add calories because they're cooked in oil, but can also upset the balance of your digestive system and aggravate a blemished skin. That's why I like fresh foods—raw fruits and vegetables mixed in salads—and foods that are cooked simply—broiled, poached, or baked in a little broth. You can't really tell your mother how to serve her dishes, but you can talk things over with her and see if you can help or surprise her with a dinner cooked a different way. Your whole family will benefit.

We all grow up hearing that good nutrition means a varied diet of healthy foods, but what does all that mean? Well, if you've been reading closely, you'll remember five important words: protein, carbohydrates, fats, vitamins, and minerals. Our bodies need all of these to keep running. Too much of one and not enough of another equals a not-so-healthy you. In a nutshell:

PROTEIN builds your muscles, with the help of vitamins and minerals.

CARBOHYDRATES give different parts of your body the energy to work, walk, run, talk.

FATS give you energy, too. (*Body* fat, however, is the end result of eating too many foods—not just butter and cream, but excess protein and carbohydrates, too.)

VITAMINS give your body the push it needs to use the other nutrients in food. They also help build your tolerance against colds and infection.

MINERALS are also body-building blocks. Calcium, only one of many minerals, is largely responsible for the formation of teeth and bones. Iron builds healthy red blood that keeps your heart working.

Most foods have more than one of these five essentials. Milk comes the closest to being a perfect food because it has a little of each: protein, carbohydrates, fat (a little in skim milk, more in whole milk), vitamins like D (which are added), and minerals like calcium.

Though each of these contributes to a healthy body, only the first three contain *calories*. A calorie is a way to measure the amount of energy-producing value in a food. If you eat a hard-boiled egg that has 70 calories, you'll have 70 calories worth of energy that will go toward building new cells or will be used up running to school or however your body decides. You use up many calories each day, about 12 to 15 for every pound you weigh, depending on how active you are. If its sounds complicated, it isn't once you know how much your body needs to keep up with the demand. If you eat a variety of foods from each of the four groups, you'll be getting all the essential nutrition you need, and you won't have to worry about taking vitamin supplements; that's something you should discuss with your doctor.

If you don't have a weight problem, you're probably eating the right amount of calories for you. But the choices you make (a candy bar vs. a piece of fruit) make all the difference between being slim and being slim and fit. Here are the portions you should have daily:

From group (1): A total of 8 to 10 ounces. This can be two eggs at breakfast, a hamburger at lunch, and a chicken cutlet at dinner.

From group (2): Two 8-ounce glasses of milk (or more), or 2 to 4 ounces of sliced cheese, or 2½ cups of cottage cheese. (If you have butter or margarine, that's extra.)

From group (3): Four slices of bread, or two rolls, or a breakfast cereal and a sandwich lunch, or two 4-ounce portions of spaghetti or potatoes or starchy vegetables like lima beans.

From group (4): Three or more servings of vegetables and three servings of fruit, like juice with breakfast, an apple with lunch, and half a grapefruit before (or after) dinner.

WHEN CALORIES START FIGURING IN YOUR FIGURE

I should know about this—a few years ago, when I was only 4 feet 11 inches, I weighed 135 pounds. I was more than overweight—I was self-conscious and uncomfortable. One day I sat myself down and said, This is ridiculous, what's more important, my figure or food? That's a question that *many* girls have to ask themselves. (If you weigh more than you like or should, don't feel that you're alone. You're not!)

This is not the way to diet!

I think the first step is setting your priorities: first figure and health, then food. You may not want to listen to me now, but one afternoon, you'll realize that no matter how pretty your face is, without a slim body below it, you won't be the same girl. I know that was true for me. As I got closer and closer to the age when I could date, I realized that I'd never attract the best kind of guy if I were heavy. And I knew I'd never feel my energetic best until I lost some weight. I can't look over your shoulder and tell you what to do every time you think of food, though I wish I could. It's an effort you're going to have to make yourself with my help.

If you're honest with yourself and unhappy about being overweight, you will decide to do something about it. It may be when you can't find anything in your closet that fits, when a kid in school calls you "Fatty," or when you look in the mirror and think you see an elephant! Did I make you smile? See, it's not as bad as all that. If I could diet and grow into a 5-feet 5-inch frame with only 95 pounds, you can find the body that's right for you too (it's there, hiding under a few extra doughnuts!).

I went on every kind of diet you can imagine: the grapefruit diet, juice diets, high-protein diets. The one that worked was a sensible one, cutting down the size of portions I ate and eliminating all junk and fattening foods (mostly desserts and fried foods). Proteins, fresh fruits and vegetables are terrific diet basics. I'm going to tell you about a diet built around them, but first, here are some ideas to get you started.

LEARN YOUR WEAKNESSES. Before you start a diet, take a notebook and write down everything you eat in a day, as well as the times and the places. At night, review your notes. Do you have a tendency to eat in the morning? At night? All through the day? Do you eat more when you're watching television? Reading or doing homework? How often do you walk into the kitchen?

Once you're aware of your habits, you can change them. If you sit down at the table and find it impossible to get up unless you've personally cleaned everyone's plate, make it a point to be excused when you've finished your serving. Your family can help by restraining your help "with the dishes" for a while. If you snack while in front of the TV, busy your hands with something else, a puzzle or a letter you write during the commercials. Keep all food out of your homework area and watch out if you find yourself staring into the "fridge" without any idea of how you got there. If you have a list of alternatives to eating, you'll be prepared to turn your attention elsewhere when the urge strikes.

When you find yourself about to spend part of your allowance on a burger and fries after school, STOP! Rush to the nearest piggy bank and make your deposit. Before you can count all the calories you've saved, you'll have enough money to buy a pretty scarf or maybe even a blouse.

SET YOUR GOALS (SLOWLY) AND YOUR REWARDS. Incentive is your best friend when you want to do anything, especially when you're trying to lose weight. Plan a short-term goal, like a 5-pound loss, rather than the whole discouraging amount, and plan a small reward once you've reached it. It doesn't have to be expensive—a hair comb or some new stationery is a nice gift for you to give yourself.

KNOW WHERE YOU ARE GOING. Though you shouldn't worry about "all that weight" you have to lose, you should have an ideal number you'd like to see register on your scale. Of course, the best way to tell when you're at the right weight is to look in the mirror and not see any bulges, but every drop in number on the scale helps.

To find your ideal weight, first determine your bone size: small (like mine), medium, or large. Do this by looking at your body in a mirror. If your hipbones, shoulders and wrists are very slim, you have a small frame. If they are wide or broad, you have a large frame. If they are in-between, yours is medium. Next multiply your height, in inches, by 1.5 if you have a small bone structure, OR 1.7 if you have a medium bone structure, OR 1.9 if you have a large bone structure. Your answer is your ideal weight. For instance: My height is 5 feet 5 inches or 65 inches. I have a small bone structure. My ideal weight is $65 \times 1.5 = 97.5$ pounds (I'm 2.5 pounds underweight!).

If you're wondering how many calories you need to maintain your weight, multiply the number of pounds by 14, the average number of calories it takes to maintain each pound under normal activity. If you're very active, use 17 instead). For me that would be $97.5 \times 14 = 1365$ calories. When you eat more calories than you burn, they are stored in reserve. Every time the extra calorie count reaches 3500, you gain one extra pound. Remember that each of your extra pounds took awhile to get there and takes even longer to go away. Be patient. It took me a year of going up and down on the scale before I had my weight under control, but it *can* be done.

CHOOSE YOUR DIET PLAN. The best (and easiest!) part of losing weight is deciding the method of dieting to use. Most girls prefer either to count calories or follow a portion guide. If you use this second plan, you don't have to worry about any decisions. And you don't take the chance of losing any nutritional value as you would if you replaced too many foods like fish and vegetables with ice cream and cookies, even in limited amounts.

THREE MEALS A DAY OR SIX? If you get hungry throughout the day and are used to snacking a lot, why not try eating six little meals a day, instead of three larger ones. I do this because my stomach is very small and gets full quickly. You can still join your family at breakfast and dinner but eat less at these times and enjoy a midday and evening mini-meal, too. The one meal you should have on time is breakfast. For a growing woman, it's crucial. Breakfast is brain food. It gets you going at the start of the day and carries you to lunch. Skipping it can mean head-aches, fatigue, and a rundown feeling.

TRY FUN INSTEAD OF FOOD. We often eat for all the wrong reasons: not because we're hungry, but because we feel bored or angry or upset or even happy. Try to find other ways to vent your emotions. If you're bored, try a new hobby. Whenever you feel the urge to eat, pick up your needlepoint. At the end of two weeks, you'll have lost two or more pounds and have a work of art, too. If you get angry or feel hurt, try to understand why and take steps to resolve the problem. If you don't have a date for the dance, try making plans with another available friend and do something completely different, which doesn't involve food.

BIG BREAKFAST, SMALL DINNER. Sounds funny, doesn't it? That's because we're used to having a small breakfast (except on special weekends) and a big dinner. But the calories we eat at dinner (and after!) don't get burned off or used as quickly as those we eat at the start of the day—they have more of a chance to turn into excess weight. That's why I always watch what I eat after four in the afternoon and enjoy myself at breakfast.

Marie's Painless Diet

BREAKFAST: 1-ounce serving of protein
                     1 serving of fruit
                     1 serving of milk
                     1 serving of bread or equivalent
                     1 serving of butter or equivalent (can be saved
                         for later)

LUNCH: 4-ounce serving of protein
                 1 serving of bread or equivalent
                 2 servings of vegetables
                 1 serving of fruit
                 1 serving of milk or equivalent (can be saved
                     for later)

DINNER: 4-ounce serving of protein
                  2 servings of vegetables
                  1 serving of fruit
                  1 serving of diet gelatin

SERVING SIZES AND CHOICES

There are six different groups taken from the basic four listed in the daily menu (fruits and vegetables count separately as do fats and dairy products). You can make up your own menus or follow this two-week sampler.

Each ounce serving of protein can be:
    1 ounce of lean meat: beef, lamb, pork, veal, chicken, turkey, liver, OR
    2 ounces of fish: tuna, salmon, sole, flounder, OR
    5 scallops, shrimps, clams, oysters or mussels, OR
    2 tablespoons of peanut butter, OR
    1 ounce of hard cheese, OR
    1 egg

Each serving of milk can be:
   One 8-ounce glass of skim milk, OR
   1-ounce slice of cheese, OR
   4 ounces of cottage cheese, OR
   1 cup plain yogurt, OR
   ½ cup of ice cream (includes 1 butter serving), OR
   ½ cup of ice milk

Each serving of bread can be:
   1 slice of whole wheat, rye or pumpernickel (better than plain
      white bread!), OR
   1 ounce of dry cereal, OR
   ⅔ cup of cooked cereal, OR
   6 saltine crackers, OR
   ½ cup of a starchy vegetable: potatoes, spaghetti or pasta,
      lentils or lima beans, corn, rice or peas, OR
   1 cup of unbuttered popcorn, OR
   1 3-inch cookie, OR
   1 hamburger or dinner roll (counts as 2 servings!)

Each serving of butter can be:
   1 teaspoon of butter, margarine, mayonnaise or salad oil, OR
   2 tablespoons of sour cream, OR
   2 teaspoons of salad dressing, OR
   1 tablespoon (½ ounce) of cream cheese

Each serving of vegetables is ½ cup of the following (those
marked with an asterisk* can be eaten in unlimited quantities):

artichokes	chives	parsley*
asparagus*	collard greens*	pumpkin
bean sprouts*	cucumbers*	radishes*
beets	eggplant	rutabaga
broccoli	green beans*	sauerkraut*
Brussels sprouts	kale	spinach*
cabbage*	lettuce*	tomatoes/tomato
carrots	mushrooms*	juice
cauliflower	okra	turnips
celery*	onions	watercress*
chard	peppers*	zucchini*

Each serving of fruit can be any of the following, but at least one should be a citrus fruit (orange, grapefruit, tangerine). Follow these proportions:
    1 small apple, pear or banana, OR
    ½ grapefruit, cantaloupe, mango or papaya, OR
    1 cup of strawberries, raspberries, blueberries, cherries or grapes, OR
    3 small apricots, OR
    1 medium orange, tangerine, nectarine or peach, OR
    2 medium plums, dates or figs, OR
    ¼ honeydew melon, OR
    1–2-inch wedge of watermelon or crenshaw melon, OR
    ½ cup of pineapple

You can also have the following foods as you wish throughout the day: diet gelatin (10 calories a serving or less), no-calorie soda, chicken, beef or vegetable bouillon (10 calories or less). Flavor salads with a little vinegar or lemon juice. Mustard, ketchup and soy sauce in small (tablespoon) amounts are okay, too.

If you stick to this diet, you can lose an average of two pounds a week. But as the weight comes off, you might notice that some weeks are better than others. At times the body hits one particular weight and refuses to budge. If that happens to you, bear with it. One morning you'll wake up and be surprised to find that a couple of pounds are gone.

Speaking of weighing yourself—don't do it too often while you're dieting. You don't want to be discouraged if the weight doesn't come off as quickly as you'd like it to. Remember how long it took me, but it was worth it! Once you reach your goal, check that scale every day (I carry mine with me whenever I'm traveling), and if you see that you've gained even 1 pound, take it off before it becomes 2 or 3 or . . .

	BREAKFAST	LUNCH	DINNER
MONDAY	1 cup rice cereal ½ cup milk (drink the rest) cantaloupe slices 1 oz. Swiss cheese	open-faced bacon, lettuce, and tomato sandwich peach halves	flounder with lemon juice green beans with butter tossed salad strawberry gelatin with fresh berries
TUESDAY	orange juice scrambled egg on toast with a little butter milk	salmon steak rice grilled tomato cucumber slices ice milk	turkey breast carrots and mushrooms baked banana slices with cinnamon
WEDNESDAY	cream of wheat with cinnamon and butter ½ melon with cottage cheese	chef's salad with 2 oz. each: turkey, ham, and cheese, on greens with tomato wedges saltines orange ice (frozen o.j. on a stick)	lamb chop with fresh mint zucchini spears green salad fresh fruit salad
THURSDAY	cheese omelette (1 egg, 1 oz. cheese) orange juice	lean hamburger on bun cole slaw pickles apple	tomato juice red snapper poached in water with herbs cauliflower rosettes small scoop of ice cream
FRIDAY	grapefruit sections peanut butter on whole wheat bread milk	chicken slices on toast carrot and celery sticks milk cherries	boiled shrimps (up to 20!) 1 tb. cocktail sauce (equal mix of horseradish + ketchup) cole slaw, tomato slices pineapple, fresh or canned in juice
SATURDAY	melted cheese on toast fruit shake (1 cup milk, 1 fruit, and 3 ice cubes liquefied in blender)	tunafish salad with chopped celery and lemon juice lettuce saltines papaya slices	sliced roast beef salad broccoli pear poached in water and vanilla flavoring

Beauty and Health: A Winning Combination

	BREAKFAST	LUNCH	DINNER
SUNDAY	roast beef on lightly buttered toast milk with blueberries	open-faced Reuben sandwich: corned beef, Swiss cheese, and sauerkraut heated under broiler tossed salad tangerine	chicken cutlet baked in chicken broth spinach and baby onions grapefruit broiled for 3 minutes
MONDAY	hard-boiled egg plain yogurt with sliced fruit	two slices pizza milk fresh fruit	chicken livers broiled with onions tossed salad gelatin with mandarin oranges
TUESDAY	cheese omelette orange juice	two pieces fried chicken (no fries!) cole slaw milk apple	lean hamburger (no roll!) green salad with tomatoes pineapple ice (crushed pineapple and juice frozen until mushy, whipped again and frozen until solid)
WEDNESDAY	two scrambled eggs honeydew melon	½ order meatballs and spaghetti milk grapes	salad bowl of tuna, cheese slices, and hard-boiled egg on lettuce with tomatoes ice milk and berries
THURSDAY	corn flakes and milk 1 oz. cheese ½ grapefruit	tunafish sandwich on whole wheat bread carrot sticks ice cream	cottage cheese and fruit green salad plums
FRIDAY	French toast (2 slices bread dipped in 1 egg) butter and 1 tb. maple syrup orange slices milk	sliced turkey and cheese on greens with tomatoes milk fresh applesauce ("no sugar added" if from jar)	fillet of sole Brussels sprouts carrots mixed melon balls

	BREAKFAST	LUNCH	DINNER
SATURDAY	cream of rice cereal with milk, cinnamon, butter grapefruit sections	eggplant parmesan (half eggplant, sliced, topped with 2 oz. ground beef, 1 oz. mozzarella, and ¼ cup tomato sauce) orange ice	broiled chicken leg peas and carrots 2 graham crackers and milk nectarines
SUNDAY	2 3-inch pancakes with berries milk	sliced chicken green beans and carrots pear halves milk	vegetable broth 2 saltines salad greens topped with meat slices baked banana with cinnamon

Ten ways to make your diet work:

1. Follow the portion guide and the menus. If the menu says: "cheese omelette," it means 1 egg and 1 ounce of cheese (substitute for milk), and no butter. When butter or its equivalent is allowed, it will say so.

2. The weekday lunches for the second week are for girls who eat lunch in school or those who have only a short break. Fast foods are tasty but also filled with calories. These suggestions allow you to get your lunch on the run but still make it "dietetic." Never buy a fattening fast-food dessert, like apple pie—it's mostly pie. Bring an apple with you from home so you don't have to skip dessert.

3. Spend $3 of your allowance on a steamer, a silver-colored, perforated tray that fits into most saucepans. This way you can steam your vegetables and fish (even fruit, like the "poached pear") over boiling water, and you won't add any calories. Here's how you or your mom can do it: Place about an inch of water in a saucepan and bring it to a boil. Then place the food on the steamer rack and ease it into the pan. Cover the pan and turn the heat down to low. In ten minutes, vegetables or fish will be done. You can even steam ground beef meatballs (for twenty minutes) to make low-calorie meatballs and spaghetti (using one bread serving, too,) and top it with a pureed tomato for sauce.

4. If you can't get fresh vegetables and fruit (hard to do in the winter unless you live in a warm climate), buy frozen or canned

ones but read the labels to make sure that no sugar or syrup has been added.

5. When broiling or baking meats or poultry, make sure all fat is trimmed off (remove all the skin from chicken and turkey). You won't be able to get the fat out from between the meat, but you can take off any surrounding fat. In the oven, place meat on a small rack within a pan so that fat can drain off as it cooks.

6. Drink plenty of water, especially before meals. Water cleanses your body and washes away any toxins. It also fills you up so you want to eat less.

7. Eat slowly and take small bites. I know you've heard this before, and no one can convince me that it makes you feel like you've eaten more, but it does make the meal last longer. If you take more time to eat, you'll finish your food at the same time everyone else has had their seconds—and you won't want to eat more all by yourself!

8. Leave something on your plate, if you can. You might feel tempted to eat later, and you can have your own leftovers. Maybe you'll save your dinner dessert until the late evening when you're watching TV and are tempted by the commercials. Remember that you can eat low-calorie gelatin anytime you want.

9. Keep a record of what you eat and when. That way you'll never be able to overeat or "accidentally" forget that you already ate your lunch serving of bread as you reach for a roll at dinner.

10. Buy a postal scale to measure portions until you can honestly judge them. It's not expensive and you'll be sure to stick to your diet.

How to Keep Your New Weight

Did you know that it's easier to lose weight than to keep it off? The real challenge of dieting is maintaining a loss. Stay on your diet for a week or two after you've reached your goal. Then, to keep from losing anymore, gradually increase the amount of food you eat. You can even treat yourself to one cookie after lunch and dinner, or maybe an afternoon scoop of ice cream (only one scoop!). Experiment cautiously for a few days. Has the scale gone back up? If it has, choose between the cookie and the ice cream (or, if you're not ice cream crazy like me, have an extra slice of meat instead of any dessert). If your weight stays the same, you know that's the most you can splurge on. But if the scale goes down a little more, you can eat a little more.

If you're the scientific type . . . you can count calories. Turn back to page 95 and figure out the calorie limit for your ideal weight. The basic diet on page 97 provides about 1200 calories a day. Use a calorie guide book to choose foods that will increase the basic diet to the amount of calories you need. My "painless" diet isn't just for losing weight; it's a diet that gives you all the essentials your body needs. By increasing the portions or adding some nondiet foods you have a *maintenance diet* (a diet that maintains or holds steady your new weight).

Some girls, who are just about 5 feet tall and have small bones, may find that 1200 calories a day is too much for them; 900 calories would be more in line with their size if they're not at all active. If that's true for you, to reach your ideal weight, you might need to cut down the portions on my diet: Have 3 ounces of protein, not 4, at lunch and dinner, and only 1 bread serving a day.

A special note for all girls:
Before you start this diet (or any diet) talk it over with your family doctor, to make sure you'll be getting all the nutrients your body needs. Some girls need more vitamins and minerals than others do, and that's something only your doctor can tell for sure.

If there's one thing I've learned about dieting and about staying in shape, it's that what you eat isn't the only factor that determines your health. Exercise is the other half of the solution to having a good figure. It tones flabby muscles and builds healthier ones. One reason we get fat is that we don't burn up all the calories we eat. So if you want to eat more (and not gain weight) or if you want to lose weight faster and look trimmer . . . exercise. Here's a whole chapter to tell you how.

8.
The Health Part: Exercise Figures In, Too!

A GREAT FIGURE isn't born—it's exercised into shape! Even girls who seem to have perfect shapes need exercise, to stay that way. Everyone has at least one problem area. What's yours? Mine's my stomach; I have a singer's diaphragm. That means I have to keep my tummy muscles in tone to keep it from sticking out! I get a lot of exercise during rehearsals (I spend a few hours each day learning all sorts of new dance steps), but I still need to practice one or two exercises that concentrate on my trouble spot.

I think it's great if you're an active, outdoors girl. But you can get in shape indoors, too. If you love skiing, swimming, playing tennis, or just plain walking, you already know that you need to warm up your body before you begin. And if you're a beginner, learning any of these or the many other great sports, *warm-up exercises* are a must. I like to do them every morning—it takes only ten or fifteen minutes—to get my whole body in gear, whether or not I'll be following it with something more strenuous. I'm not a super athlete, but I still enjoy sports. I play football with my family; I love swimming and horseback riding; I've even tried baseball and I like it, although my game is not worth beans.

These exercises will help you get in shape because they tone the different parts of your body. Even if you're dieting, bumps and bulges may not go away without exercise. As with dieting, you have to be patient; you won't see results overnight.

Practice each of these in the morning, before you start your skin-care and makeup routine, *and* in the evening, if you're really in a hurry to see results.

Marie's Figure-Perfect Exercises

For the arms:

1. Stand up straight with your feet slightly apart for better balance. Stretch your arms out to the sides, palms up. Now rotate your arms, from the socket under the arm to the hands,

in small, clockwise circles, twenty times, then twenty times counterclockwise. Repeat the whole exercise, making larger circles in both directions.

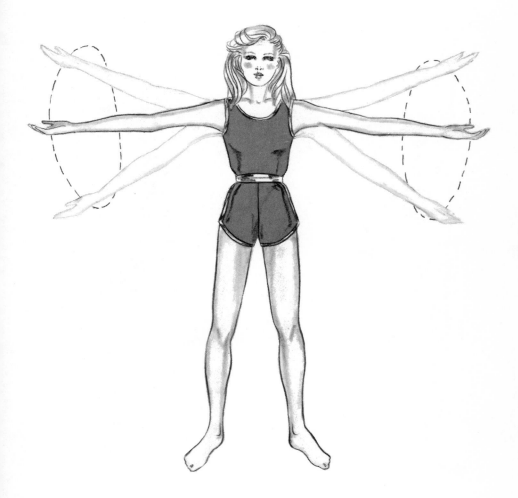

2. Turn your feet outward and space them wide apart. Raise your arms over your head and turn your palms inward so they face each other. Now tilt your body, from the waist up only, to the left, as far as you can go. Return your torso to the center and repeat four more times. Then repeat the exercise to the right. Your arms move with your body, keeping parallel to each other.

For your torso:

3. Standing in the same position, fold your arms and cup each elbow with the hand of the other arm. Slowly raise your folded arms over and in back of your head and bounce them toward the wall behind you five times. Return your arms to your chest and repeat the exercise four more times.

4. Now lie down, with your tummy flat on the floor (on a blanket or an exercise mat, if you have one), and do fifteen push-ups. Start by raising your feet on your toes (heels are in the air). Raise your chest off the floor by straightening your arms, palms flat on the floor at shoulder level. If this beginning position is too difficult for you, your legs can be flat as you push up only your upper torso. Lower and raise your body (or chest only) by bending your arms at the elbows and then straightening them. As they straighten, they *push* your body *up*.

For your hips:

5. Roll over on your back and stretch your arms out to the sides. Bend your knees together toward your chest. Keeping your upper torso flat on the floor, roll your hips to the right so that your right knee almost touches the floor. Return to center and repeat to the left, left knee touching the floor. Return to center and repeat seven times to both sides.

6. In the same starting position, bend your right leg, foot flat on the floor. Raise your left leg to a 90-degree angle to your body, knee straight, and rotate it in a large circle without touch-

ing the floor. Circle to the right, then down and around to the left, then back up. Do five times in one direction, then five times in the other. Repeat the whole exercise with the right leg.

For your thighs:

7. Lie on your right side now, leaning on your right elbow and placing your left hand in front of your chest, flat on the floor, for support. Lift you left leg about 8 inches from the floor and hold it. Raise your right leg and touch it to your left foot. Return the right leg to the floor and then your left one. Repeat this nine more times; then turn over and do it all again on the left side.

8. Lie flat on your back with your legs flat in front of you. Lift your back from the floor and hold yourself up with your elbows. Point your toes and bring your left knee toward your chest. Keeping your right leg straight out on the floor, straighten the left one, lifting it toward your left ear as far as it can go without straining. Bend it again and repeat seven more times; then switch to the right leg, going toward your right ear.

For your stomach:

9. Lie on your back on the floor, with your knees bent and your feet flat on the floor. Stretch your arms in front of you and do ten half sit-ups, raising your back halfway off the floor. Pull yourself up by pulling in and tightening your stomach muscles, not by pulling with your arms.

10. Lie flat, arms at your sides. Simultaneously, lift your head, shoulders, your right arm and your left leg off the floor, reaching toward your left foot with your right hand. Pull in your stomach muscles as you go. Relax, slowly, to the floor and switch to the left arm and the right leg. (Your head and shoulders, but not your back, lift every time.) Alternate for a total of twenty times.

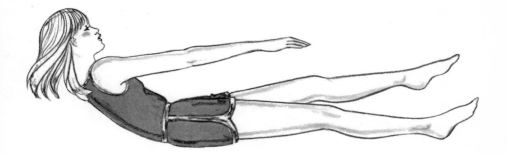

For your waist:

11. Sit up and spread your legs into a wide "V." Raise your arms over your head and bending from your waist, make a sweeping circle with your torso: Bend to the right, then toward your feet, to the left and back up again. Repeat this four more times, then five times in the other direction.

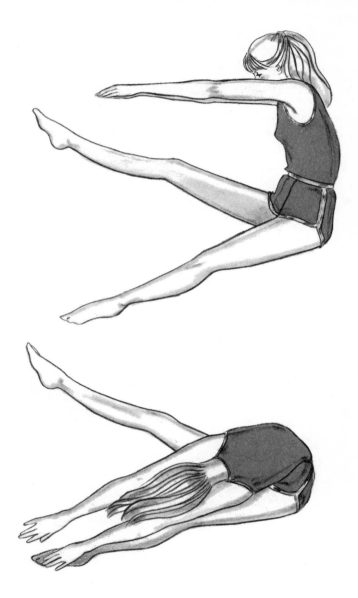

12. Now stand up straight and bend over from the waist. This last exercise is called the "windmill" because your arms swing like those of the Dutch mill. With your feet wide apart, swing your right hand to touch your left foot and at the same time, raise your left arm over your head past the shoulder, keeping your eyes and head turned to face it. Now swing the left arm down to the right foot and raise your right arm past your shoulder. Once you get the rhythm of the exercise, shift arms twenty times. (To tighten stomach at the same time, keep these muscles contracted.) Now, still bent over, pull in your stomach muscles and straighten your back from the waist up; don't lead with your head. Feel each little vertebra in your spine straighten, then your shoulders, and then your head. Take a few deep breaths and . . . you're done. Was that so hard?

You've just limbered up your body and prepared it for a busy day.

If you take a gym class at school, you might want to ask your instructor for her ideas on trouble spot exercises or incorporate some of those you do in school with your at-home ones. If you don't have a coach to give you incentive, try rounding up a group of your friends on weekends and holding your own exercise class. You can get pointers from professionals through the use of records or cassettes and booklets that describe their techniques. Your local record store could probably get one of these for you. If not, you can write to them directly for more information:

- Marjorie Craig's 21 Day Shape-up Plan (Elizabeth Arden Salon, 691 Fifth Avenue, New York, N.Y. 10022)
- Jazzercise (Box 1414, Vista, Calif. 92083)
- The Nickolaus Technique (Nickolaus Exercise Tape, 509 Fifth Avenue, New York, N.Y. 10017)

The Active Girl

I know she's hiding there somewhere—there's a little of her in all of us. If you take a look at the calorie-burning sports chart on

PHOTOCRAFT

the next page to see how many extra calories you can exercise away while having lots of fun, I'm sure you'll find her.

The Calorie-Burning Activity Chart

ACTIVITY	CALORIES BURNED IN 1 HOUR
Sleeping/resting in bed	60
Eating	65
Dressing	150
Ping-Pong	180
Baseball	210
Housework/chores	215
Walking 3 miles	240
Dancing	250
Swimming	250
Volleyball	265
Calisthenics/gymnastics	300
Horseback riding, trotting	320
Basketball	325
Ice-skating/roller-skating	350
Bicycling 10 miles	360
Jumping rope	400
Tennis, singles	420
Skiing	450
Jogging	480
Running	550–600

At school, you're probably able to play most of the team sports: volleyball, basketball, maybe even swimming and tennis. Gymnastics, using the parallel bars and other gym equipment, are fun too. Lots of other activities that you do for fun, like biking, can really improve your shape. All you need is a routine that you can stick to at least three times a week, plus your morning exercises. On the following pages, I'll tell you about some great sports activities that are easy to learn.

On your mark—Before you start any sport (and even your exercises), you should make sure that you're wearing the right clothes for that activity. Even more important is that you are

PHOTOCRAFT

comfortable. If you hair is long, tie it back but alternate, each day, among a ponytail, braids, barrettes . . . so that your hair isn't pulled or stretched in one direction. Except for walking, you should have on only a minimum of makeup or none at all. Exercises really get you moving and that means you'll perspire. Perspiration and makeup add up to—a mess! But for outdoor exercise, remember to protect your delicate facial skin and any other exposed areas with the correct product—sunscreen, moisturizer, lip balm.

Get set—Just as the morning exercises get you ready for the whole day, they can prepare you for any other activity. Do them

Ready, set, go! PHOTOCRAFT

124

four times each, instead of eight, before you go riding or biking or whatever. They stretch your muscles and warm them, preventing cramps or a charley horse.

Go—Pick your favorite from those listed on the chart. The columns will tell you what you need to begin, what to wear, how often to do it, and for how long. It takes practice to learn a new sport, just like any skill, and the more you do it, the better you'll be—and look. Keep up with your sports schedule, once you're in the best possible shape, to keep you that way.

SPORT	HOW TO BEGIN	WHAT TO WEAR/ EQUIPMENT	HOW OFTEN/ FOR HOW LONG
BICYCLING	Start with a 2-mile ride in your neighborhood—in case you run out of energy! Build up to 10-20 miles at an easy pace.	Close-fitting but not tight clothes: T-shirt and shorts in summer; straight-leg pants and a pullover in fall/ spring. Use a visor to shield your eyes from the sun; sunscreen on exposed skin.	Two or three times a week, not just on weekends; start with 10–15 minutes, build to an hour or more. It's easier and more fun with a friend.
CALISTHENICS	Add to your morning exercises (yes, they are called calisthenics!) with others from magazines or TV exercise programs or records.	A T-shirt and shorts, or a leotard and tights without feet to give you better traction on the floor. For floor exercises, put down a mat or blanket if floor is not carpeted.	Build up your 15-minute routine to ½ hour or even 45 minutes, three or more times a week. If you have calisthenics at school, really make an effort to do well.
DANCING	Put on a favorite record and move with the music (it can be slow or fast). Buy a book of ballet steps and practice them, using a sturdy chair for balance. Watch a dance performance on television and move with the performers.	Flexible clothing. But even if you disco, don't wear your dancing shoes!	Progress from a 45 rpm to an LP! Try dancing a little every afternoon to build up your endurance. Think about taking a professional dance class twice a week.

125

SPORT	HOW TO BEGIN	WHAT TO WEAR/ EQUIPMENT	HOW OFTEN/ FOR HOW LONG
JUMPING ROPE	Start with ten jumps and build up by tens. If you find yourself skipping over the rope instead of jumping, practice making little jumps without the rope.	A leotard and footless tights, or tights with sneakers will give you the best traction; shorts, T-shirt, and sneakers if outside. A nylon braided rope with ball-bearing handles is the most durable.	Each jump takes about 2 seconds; build up to 10 minutes and practice every day. You can try for more, but it's one of the few sports that gets boring!
RUNNING	Start in your neighborhood at an easy pace, and as you build up tolerance, increase your pace. This is the most strenuous exercise of all.	A running or sweat suit will keep you well insulated, but in summer, shorts and a T-shirt are often enough. Good sneakers (running shoes) are extra important.	Start with 5 to 10 minutes. Gradually build up to 30 minutes twice or three times a week.
SWIMMING	This is a great sport to learn for your health and for a lot of fun. Your can even do most of your daily exercises in the water for extra benefit. Get lessons at your local Y —it's worth it!	A one-piece swimsuit without ties or bows to worry about coming undone, or a well-constructed leotard made for swimming. (After every swim, wash your hair to rinse out chlorine from the pool.)	Start with 10 laps and increase to 30 or 60. You can alternate different strokes—the sidestroke uses more calories than the crawl. If you school doesn't have a pool, join the Y and work out two to three times a week. (Other activities might be included in the fee.)
WALKING	Start by walking to school, if it's about a mile away. Walk at a brisk pace, not one used for window-shopping. Next time you have an appointment, walk to it instead of going by car or bus.	Comfortable clothes and shoes—don't wear high heels if you're going to do a lot of walking.	Walk as often and as long as you can. It's great and doesn't require anything but a little energy.

126

These activities require little equipment or money. But there are many other kinds of exercise. Some are studied as an art—ballet, fencing, yoga—and others are practical only for limited occasions—canoeing, snowshoeing, snowmobiling. Pastimes like golf, bowling, tennis, racquetball, squash, riding, and skiing can cost more (lessons, rental fees, transporation), but they're lots of fun. If you're not sure which one is for you, talk it over with your gym instructor or go to the library and read through a book describing a sport you think you might like. The choice is yours!

9.
The Health Part:
Take Good Care of Yourself

SOMETIMES, WHEN WE'RE concerned with taking all the right steps to beauty, we forget about our health; we take it for granted. We put on lipstick, to make our smile prettier, and we forget about our teeth. We buy lots of new colors of eyeshadow . . . and overlook our eyes. I get so busy doing ten different things at once that I forget about getting the proper rest and treating myself to something nice and simple, like a warm bubble bath. These are some of the most important steps to beauty, frequently pushed aside because the effort we take in doing them often goes unnoticed. But if your teeth aren't sparkling and your eyes aren't shining, can you really be your prettiest self?

Caring for Your Teeth—the Osmond Trademark!

Mother says we get our teeth from Father's side of the family. And we smile so much to show them off because of all the years spent making them perfect—we've all worn braces or retainers! I wore them for four years, but I'm glad that I did. Until my teeth were all straightened, I felt like I had a vampire's smile! It's okay to joke about it now, but I felt very inferior then. There's nothing worse than not wanting to participate in a conversation because you're inhibited by your teeth. And I've seen lots of girls lose their personality because they would constantly cover their mouth with their hands or withdraw altogether. If you have buck teeth or even one tooth that's out of line, talk it over with your parents and your dentist who can probably recommend a specialist—an orthodontist—to correct the problem. (If he's too

Showing off the Osmond family trademark with my brother Donny.

expensive, you may be able to go to a teaching college of dentistry and be cared for by a graduating student, under the guidance of a professional.)

Whether you need braces or were blessed with straight teeth, care doesn't stop here or with your toothbrush. Because of all the nooks and crevices in between teeth, cleaning the surfaces with your toothbrush isn't enough. Dental plaque that develops when bacteria mixes with trapped food particles causes cavities

129

and can also cause an infection of your gums, called gingivitis. To stop this plaque from hardening as it mixes with minerals in your saliva and attacking your teeth by eating away at its calcium, it has to be removed once a day. This care prevents problems that make you afraid of going to the dentist. Brushing twice a day or more (whenever you want to freshen your mouth) is great, but at night, before you go to sleep, your toothbrush needs the help of three other workers to keep your teeth and gums healthy forever: dental floss, and dental stimulator, and disclosing liquid.

Unwaxed dental floss is a thick threadlike fiber that is worked in between teeth and under the gumline to gently scrape off bacterial plaque. Be sure the floss is unwaxed; the waxed kind doesn't do as thorough a job.

The *dental stimulator* gently massages gums to increase circulation and make them healthier and stronger. Weak gums cause teeth to fall out.

Disclosing liquid turns plaque red so that you can see where it collects in your mouth, and you'll know when you've removed all of it. Unlike the other instruments, it's not something you'll have to use every night, but only until you learn to thoroughly clean your teeth.

This routine can really be boring, but it will become less of a bother once you get used to it. And I think that a few minutes at night is worth having beautiful teeth—ask any Osmond!

1. Floss between all your teeth. Snap off a piece about two feet long and wrap it around your left middle finger. Take the loose end and twist it around your right one. Unwind about 2 inches from the left hand as you go in between every two teeth, starting at the upper right corner of your mouth and wrapping it around the right finger as it is used. Use your thumbs to steady the floss and work it up and down along the sides of each tooth. Use your index fingers when working on the lower teeth. You'll see that at the sides of every tooth the gum forms a loose flap: slip the floss just under the gum to remove any particles hiding here. If you need more floss, repeat the winding process with fresh thread. Practice in front of a mirror until you learn the technique. If you notice some bleeding, use a lighter touch. If the bleeding is more profuse and gums look red and swollen, see your dentist right away.

2. Swoosh a few drops of disclosing liquid around your teeth or chew up a disclosing tablet. Look in the mirror—but don't faint. It will look strange, especially if you didn't floss well. Snap off another piece of floss and use it to remove the red-colored plaque in between teeth.

3. Brush your teeth, covering only three or four teeth with each stroke from the gum to the crown of the teeth, not just a quick, straight back-and-forth motion. Brush the front side of the top teeth and then the back side. Repeat this with your lower teeth. Now brush the top surfaces of the teeth where many cavities form. If you like to use toothpaste, you can use it now and go over all the teeth with a circular motion. (*Note:* If you notice that plaque or a whitish film forms on your tongue, brush it gently, too—this is a very common thing and there's nothing wrong with brushing here.)

4. Examine your teeth closely. See any red color left? Floss again. By now it should all be gone, and you should be aware of your trouble spots.

5. Once you've cleaned your mouth, it's time to use the dental stimulator. You've probably seen a pink rubber tip at the end of many toothbrushes—that's a dental stimulator. But it's better to buy a separate instrument with a sturdy metal handle. The pointy pink tip is placed between teeth and rotated in a gentle circular motion to tone the gums. After ten little circles, move to the next tooth in the same direction you've flossed.

Water Piks do this job with sprays of water that get in between the teeth. Ask your dentist about using one.

It's probably taken you a few minutes to read about the different steps, but it will be as natural to you as washing your face in a matter of days. You also won't have to rely on candylike breath fresheners, which only temporarily mask the sour odor of bad breath that comes from this bacterial plaque.

It's important to care for your teeth on your own, but it's still important to visit your dentist. He can check on your at-home work and examine your teeth for signs of trouble you might not be able to recognize. Every six months.

Caring for Your Eyes

Your eyes are your most important beauty feature, and your vision is the most important of your five senses. Because you ask them to do a double job, you should treat them with extra care.

Getting enough sleep isn't always enough to soothe tired eyes. If you've been doing a lot of reading or close work, like embroidery or painting, or watching hour after hour of television, give them one evening's rest (no, that doesn't mean you should ignore your homework, but after it's finished—). To cool tired eyes, close them and cover each lid with a cold slice of cucumber! Eye drops will clear redness, but don't rely on them every day.

To prevent eye problems, protect eyes from the sun (even in winter), the wind, and bad weather. The best way to do that is to shield them, with sunglasses, goggles, or a visor (good when you're participating in active sports). Goggles offer protection in very bad wind and snow, as well as on the slopes. Sunglasses are the most useful and frequently used of the three, year round. Did you know that the sun's reflection on snow in the winter can be as uncomfortable as the strong summer sun? Sunglasses will protect your eyes from the glare and from snow-blindness —sunburn of the eyes.

Though you may not need a prescription for them, you should choose sunglasses with the same concern as you would regular glasses.

FRAMES

Frames should complement your face and conform to the shape of your eyebrows so that you don't have two sets of frames for your eyes. Pretty frames can really flatter you and be a distinctive part of your personality. One pair of my frames is even tinted rose with lenses that match. They're prescription ones that work as regular and *sun*glasses because the tint on the lenses is dark at the top, going to pale and clear at the bottom.

Here are some tips for getting the right frames:

Wearing pretty frames is fun—and can be a great fashion accessory.   PHOTOCRAFT

- Choose plastic frames tinted in a soft color like rose, mauve, apricot, a neutral, pale olive, or blue. Opaque colors like white or black look too obvious; they really stand out. Frames should work as part of your makeup. Just as you choose shades of eyeshadow to complement your eye color, so should you choose a frame tint.
- Try to stay away from metal frames that add extra weight and can leave red impressions on the bridge of your nose. Plastic

133

lenses are safer and lighter than glass—that'll help cut down on the pressure as well.

- If your old glasses have become uncomfortable or if new ones are taking too long for you to adjust to, have your frames checked by your optometrist.
- Frames can camouflage a less-than-perfect bone structure: If your face is very full and round, try geometric-shaped frames with interesting angles; if your face is squarish, try oval or round frames.

CONTACT LENSES

I think that glasses can be a fashion accessory, especially sunglasses. But if you don't like eyeglasses, why not try contact lenses? "Contacts" used to be very expensive, but now a pair is often no more costly than a pair of frames and lenses. For as long as they've existed, there's been a debate between hard and soft lenses—which ones are better. Some people, who don't seem to adjust quickly to hard lenses, have found they're able to wear soft ones, but the soft ones are more expensive. Whichever you decide to get, you and the specialist who is fitting them should have an agreement that you're buying them on a trial basis. That means if you can't adjust to them, you can return them. (Most reputable opticians won't try to sell you a pair until they're sure you can wear them.) Contact lenses require special solutions for storing (in a special case) and for *wetting* or putting them on, so you'll have to consider their upkeep (and they're a lot harder to find than a misplaced pair of glasses!).

Because particles of dust and makeup can cause an eye irritation when they touch the lens, you'll need to wear nonwaterproof mascara that will dissolve in the eye if it flakes. (Waterproof flakes will lodge in the eye, and the lens will have to be removed, rinsed, and reinserted.)

Contacts, unlike tinted eyeglasses, aren't a replacement for sunglasses, but you will be able to wear the less-expensive nonprescription sunglasses when you wear your lenses.

Whether you opt for glasses or contacts, you'll need to have them fitted by a professional. There are different yet similar sounding names for eye specialists; you should know each: An *Ophthalmologist* is a medical doctor who specializes in the care of the eyes and should be visited once a year. He'll send you to an *Optician* who fills the prescription for glasses. He doesn't measure you for them, but he can make them for you. An *Optometrist* can examine your eyes and write out the prescription for glasses or lenses, but he can't perform medical services, like writing medicinal prescriptions. He can re-evaluate your lenses every year, but he can't perform other tests that are included in the ophthalmologist's examination.

Special beauty note: Remember that the skin around your eyes is very delicate. Even if eyes are red and itchy, don't rub them. Soothe them with cold-water cotton compresses, followed by eye cream, dabbed on with your pinkie, below the lower lashes.

A Little Bit of Luxury—the Bubble-Plus Bath

Mornings are a great time to take a quick shower—that's usually all there's time for! But to relax and feel really pampered and a little bit special, there's nothing like a fragrant bubble bath.

Ordinary bubbles that add only color to the water aren't for you any more. Because one or two nights a week is usually all the time you have for the full treatment, the potions you put in your bath have to do a special job. Here are just a few of the terrific bath beautifiers to add to warm (not hot; that's too much of a shock to your system) water as you're filling the tub:

- *Milk baths*—powdered bubbles that contain milk and perfume for a nourishing bath. You can mix your own by pouring in a packet of powdered milk (a lot less expensive than a whole quart!), a capful of baby oil, and a few drops of perfume.
- *Bath gels*—a glycerine-based water softener with bubbles and scent.
- *Bath salts*—Epsom salts will give you a refreshing feeling, especially if you've been on your feet all day (and they're inexpensive, too!)
- *Bath oil*—no bubbles, but lots of conditioners to soften your skin.

And while you're in the tub:
Use a *natural sponge* or *mitt* to lather with a *glycerine bar* (if your skin's normal to oily) *or a superfatted* soap (if it's dry); a *loofah sponge*, which looks like a piece of shredded wheat, to gently scrub off dead skin cells and give your skin a healthy glow as it improves circulation.

After your bath:
- Use a *fluffy bath sheet* or a *terrycloth robe* to soak up water and then buff yourself dry.
- Slather on a good all-purpose *body lotion or cream,* on dry areas like your elbows, knees, ankles, and hands.
- Use a large, soft *puff* to dab yourself with *talc* (baby powder with a fresh scent or perfumed dusting powder if you've started using fragrance).

If you're usually rushed in the morning, use these extra minutes at night to do your mani/pedicure, tweeze your brows, or give yourself a mini-facial with the recipe for your skin type, described in chapter 2. Afterward you'll be relaxed and refreshed and ready for a nice long sleep.

Sweet Dreams

Sleep time is beauty time, too. If you don't get enough or if you get too much, your whole body gets out of whack. And the first to show the bad effects is your skin, your foundation for beauty. It starts to lack tone, and the thin skin around your eyes appears darker because of strained blood vessels. You lack energy to do your exercises, get a good breakfast, even get through the day. Too much sleep can leave you feeling sluggish, too, because it takes longer to warm up your muscles—and once you start feeling lazy, it starts to feel very familiar and comfortable. I think it's great to spend a whole day in bed once in a while—it's great to fast on juices for one day a month, too, but if you did it every day, you'd be in pretty bad shape.

It's hard to believe that we each spend one third of our life asleep—our body needs all that time to recuperate from the first sixteen hours of the day! Some people can get away with six or seven hours; others need as much as nine or ten, though the average is eight. How much sleep do you need?

To find out what's best for you, keep a record of what time you go to sleep and when you wake up on weekdays and weekends. (Remember to mark down the time you awake, not the time you get out of bed.) Does the number of hours slept vary? On what mornings did you feel most refreshed? When you figure out which sleep time is best for you, try to stick to it. Calculate the time you should go to sleep by counting backward the number of hours you need from the time you have to get up. Example: If you have to get up at 7:30 AM, and you need eight-and-a-half hours sleep, go to bed at 11 PM.

Sometimes I can't wait until nighttime to fall asleep. If I've

There's nothing like a nap after a long, busy day.   PHOTOCRAFT

had a very busy or hectic day, I find that a short nap is terrific, especially if I have an important date that evening. No makeup in the world can make you look as well as twenty minutes of rest. Even if you don't think you can fall asleep, you can lie down, with your feet propped up under a pillow. But set your alarm, just in case. Any more than twenty minutes, and you may not want to get up again.

There are other nights when I feel that I just can't fall asleep, even if I was up at 6 AM for an early rehearsal. If this happens to you, try some of these ideas that have helped me:

- Check the thermostat in your room. If the temperature's too high, you may have trouble falling asleep. And once you are asleep, and your body temperature has risen, you may wake yourself up when trying to kick off your covers. The best and most comfortable temperature is about 64 degrees, just a shade cooler than the daytime one of 68 degrees. You also might want to open a window, just a quarter of an inch. Fresh air is conducive to sleep.
- Find your most comfortable position when lying down. People who sleep on their stomach or side usually toss and turn a lot, or wake up with cramps or a strained neck. Try sleeping on your back with a small pillow under your head and neck where you need support. Or try it without a pillow—you may be surprised.
- Do a little nighttime daydreaming about something special— not about tomorrow's math test! Thinking about problems in the dark can really make them seem worse, but thinking about a dance, a new dress, or a holiday can relax and put you into a peaceful sleep.
- If you really don't feel sleepy, even though it's bedtime, do something that's not too strenuous, but will give you a feeling of having accomplished an important task: Write a long over-due letter, sort out your desk drawer, do a little advance home-work. The bad thing to do is to exercise: That much physical activity will lift you up and keep you awake longer. If you want to do your exercises at night, do them before you wash your face and floss your teeth.
- If all else fails, don't forget that a glass of warm milk (skim, if you're on a diet, "hot chocolate" made from carob if you're

not) still works: The calcium it contains has a relaxing effect on your nervous system!

Beauty and health—there's a lot to learn, and a lot to do every morning to be sure the world sees only your best self. Yes, beauty is a routine, but it's one that makes you feel as good as you look.

10.

Memo from Marie:
62 Minutes to Get Ready!

WHEN I WAS little, it seemed that all I had to do every morning was brush my teeth, splash my face with water, and brush my hair—about four minutes of getting ready, since I had had my bath the night before. But not any more—now it seems as though there's never enough time to do everything I know I should. That's why I decided to sit down with paper and pen and write out all the morning essentials and how long I would need to do them. I found little ways of saving time—like washing my face (the first step in skin care) in the shower and plugging in my electric rollers beforehand, so that they'd be ready when I was.

Keeping to my schedule isn't always easy, but it helps to prepare some things the night before: make sure you know what you'll be wearing before you go to sleep (check for missing buttons, ironing, etc.), tweeze your eyebrows, if you need to, after you've washed your face and do any de-fuzzing then, too.

Marie's Morning Schedule

FOR YOUR:	HERE'S WHAT TO DO:	TIME ALLOWED:	FOR MORE INFO SEE:
BODY	The morning exercises, all 12!	10 minutes at a quick pace	chapter 8
TEETH	Brush them thoroughly; use a freshening toothpaste/mouthwash*	3 minutes	chapter 9 and following note*
BODY	Take a quick shower; wash your face, leaving lather on while you lather your body. If you're going to use electric rollers, plug them in *before* you get in and keep them far away from the water.	3 minutes; 5, if you shampoo, too	chapter 2 (4, if necessary)
	Next, briskly towel dry and apply deodorant* under arms, body lotion all over to put back your body's softening oils. If you use powder/perfume, apply them now.	3 minutes	chapter 5, and following note*
EYES	If they're tired or red, use eye drops and close them for 30 seconds.	1 minute total	chapter 9
SKIN	Use astringent or toner and moisturizer as directed for your skin type.	1 minute	chapter 2
HAIR	If you've shampooed it, blow it dry, and if you style it with rollers, put the heated ones in now or use a curling iron.	5 minutes to blow dry; 3 minutes to set in rollers	chapter 4
FACE	Apply your makeup while hair's being set: blusher, mascara, and gloss for day. If you need and use coverage apply foundation/powder first.	4 minutes, 7 with all steps	chapter 3
NAILS	Check them for any chips and polish as needed.	4 minutes, including drying time	chapter 5
HAIR	Rollers are carefully removed; hair is combed out. Brush it into place or use hair combs. A simple style is best for daytime.	5 minutes	chapter 4

FOR YOUR:	HERE'S WHAT TO DO:	TIME ALLOWED:	FOR MORE INFO SEE:
CLOTHES	With your clothes all chosen, you should be able to slip quickly into them; but be careful if you wear hose that can easily rip on a fingernail or a zipper. Before you leave your room, quickly make your bed, hang up clothes.	5 minutes	chapter 11
ENERGY	Breakfast on the run: see the quick, nourishing breakfasts following.	10 minutes	chapter 7 for dieters' menus
TOTAL		52 to 62 minutes for everything!	

Special notes for you:

Using deodorants and products like mouthwash is fine, as long as you're not using them to mask an odor. If you really clean your mouth, you probably won't need a mouthwash. Deodorants can be helpful if you have a strong tendency to perspire; in fact, an antiperspirant might even be better for you. The first discourages odor, the second discourages its cause: perspiration.

Start your day with a quick shower, especially after exercise, to wash away any odor-causing perspiration. Apply baby powder after the shower to keep you cool and if that's not enough, try one of the deodorants.

Breakfasts on the Run

Here are five quick meals, for Monday through Friday, days when you won't have much time to linger at the table.

MONDAY: Fresh fruit drink. In blender, combine 8 oz. of milk with ¼ cup pineapple chunks, 1 whole banana and 1 raw egg. Drink up your breakfast! (On occasion, I also add one tablespoon of soybean protein powder.)

TUESDAY: Squeeze a glass of fresh orange juice while you toast an English muffin. Spread the muffin with peanut butter (full of protein) and honey or natural fruit preserves.

WEDNESDAY: Arrange two slices each of roast beef and cheese on black bread. Enjoy this Danish style breakfast with a big glass of milk.

THURSDAY: Have a glass of tomato juice with a cheese omelette. Pour the fork-stirred eggs onto a very hot nonstick pan. Top with thin pieces of cheese. Fold half the eggs over the rest, flip and let them cook for 1 minute longer.

FRIDAY: Blend 2 oz. of honey with 3 apricots and 8 oz. of orange juice in a mixer until liquefied. Drink this and eat 2 hard-boiled eggs, cooked the night before.

These breakfasts are a great end to a busy to get-ready schedule and an even better beginning to a busier day!

Fashion Savvy

IN the first chapter of this book, I said that class really makes a girl stand out in a crowd. Making the most of your beauty is one part of it; how you act is another. And the third essential ingredient is the way you dress.

Someone once said that clothes make the man. Well, I'm not sure how concerned guys are with clothes for themselves, but one thing I've learned from eight brothers is that they notice what girls are wearing! And one of the things my brothers have in common—aside from music, naturally—is that they don't like sloppy dressing. T-shirts and jeans are fun and they have their place, but for school, work, dates, and certainly special occasions, you need a more complete wardrobe. Fashion savvy can enable you to extend a few separates and a lot of accessories into a big wardrobe that will spell good taste in every situation.

And that's class!

11.
Fashion Savvy: The Clothes Closet

CAN YOU DESCRIBE your personality to me? Are you the country girl who likes casual, sporty clothes? Are you a very feminine young lady who likes frills and lace, soft, delicate fabrics? Are you the sophisticated type who likes to wear the latest styles and set the trend for everyone else? If you're like me —and most girls—you're a little bit of all of these and more: You have your own style, and can make the clothes in your closet look different on you than on any other girl who's wearing them. The most important characteristic you can develop, in terms of fashion and practically everything else, is good taste and a sense of yourself.

Do you have an objective eye? You do if, after trying on the latest cut in pants, for instance, you decide that they don't flatter your shape—even if they are the hottest look this season.

Fashion looks are divided into the four seasons of nature. However, all designers and magazines "preview" their new styles as early as three to four months before the weather permits us to wear them.

I try to stay up on fashion trends and so should you, but you have to be very choosy—*you* must wear your clothes, they can't wear you. When you read fashion magazines, remember the advice I gave you about makeup trends: Tailor the looks you like to suit you. Magazines try to create a sensation with everything new that comes along; they show extreme examples of new looks in order to be controversial and sell more magazines. If I like the idea behind a fashion layout, I find a way of interpreting it for me. Like the tuxedo shirt—a woman's version of a man's formal shirt that "everyone" seemed to be wearing—many with full tuxedos to go with it. I liked the look, especially the neat shoelace tie worn around the collar. But to buy the whole outfit

—an expensive suit that "no one" will be wearing in a few months—would be crazy. So I bought one of the shirts and teamed it up with a pair of straight leg pants and a double wrap belt. This outfit is more in keeping with my at-home lifestyle (unlike the complete tux outfit!).

Good taste is a combination of knowing what's appropriate for your lifestyle (like my decision above) and knowing how to wear the clothes you have with a distinctive flair. Some girls think that having a full wardrobe means having a new outfit for every day of the month. Other girls equate being fashionable with having enough money to buy all the "in" fashions every season. Neither of these beliefs is guaranteed to give you style. In the first case, you don't need thirty outfits to have thirty different looks. Instead, you can combine varied blouses with a couple of pants or skirts and accessorize them, as well as dresses and suits, so that they look a little bit different each time you wear them. And in the second case, being able to buy all the new clothes doesn't mean you can make them look right on you. My mother has a saying about fashion: There are two ways you can dress— you can follow the newest styles and look trendy, or you can be true to yourself and look classy and chic. If you know me, you'll know which way I dress. I like to buy clothes that will last, that have classic styling. It doesn't matter if you have to start slowly; you'll always be able to combine the new purchases with the old because classic styles are never out-of-date. That's why it makes sense to spend a little more on quality: better fabrics, better construction. I can still wear clothes I bought five years ago because of their traditional design: simple lines and tailoring. And that doesn't mean they look matronly. They look as great today as they did when I bought them. Sure I have some fun, trendy pieces to use as accents, but the main part of my closet is a collection of clothes that will last indefinitely. For the same amount of money, I'd rather have a soft knit sweater that can be worn with everything than a handkerchief-point tunic (a trendy piece) that will look right only over a simple pair of black pants —not a tweed pair, not a skirt, only one pair of pants.

It's hard to know where and how to start putting together your first important wardrobe. There are many things to consider: what you already have, what you most badly need, what kind of clothes fit most of your activities (like school and casual dates).

Start by opening your closet—now's as good a time as any to face it. Make a list with different columns like this one:

PANTS	SKIRTS	SWEATERS	SHIRTS	BLOUSES	DRESSES

Write down everything that still fits and is in good condition. Talk to your mom about donating the rest to a church or a charity. Now fill in the holes. Which pants and skirts lack matching or coordinated shirts or sweaters? Do you have a pretty lacy shirt, but nothing to wear it with? With what will you replace those too small pants—the ones that went with your tweedy sweater? Make another list, with all the separates you need to work with those you have and place a number next to each one, starting with the most sorely needed.

Appropriateness is an important part of good taste. You can't be your best if you're not wearing the right clothes at the right time. Being underdressed or overdressed is the wrong way to stand out in a crowd. One of my best-kept dating principles is to know where you're going before the date: first, because your parents should know where you'll be, and second, so that you'll know what to wear. If you're going to a restaurant, find out how fancy it is—no, it doesn't have to be the best place in town, but if it is, you should know it so that you can put on your best dress outfit.

149

Basic Components

If you're starting from scratch, don't despair. You can have a terrific wardrobe with only a dozen basic pieces that will give you dozens of different looks for all occasions: school or work, play, casual and dressy dates. The twelve separates that I suggest can be combined to suit all the different occasions in your life. You can repeat them in winter fabrics and summer ones. (In most cities, the winter clothes can be worn into spring and then again at the beginning of the fall; summer selections can be worn from late spring into fall.)

(WINTER FABRIC/SUMMER FABRIC)

1) **Pants:** a wool/linen blend
2) **Pants:** velvet/crepe de chine polyester
3) **Pants:** corduroy/cotton denim jeans
4) **Skirt:** wool/challis
5) **Skirt:** tweed/jersey blend
6) **Shirt-jacket:** to match all three pairs of pants
7) **Blouson or lacy blouse**
8) **Tailored shirt** (more than one if possible): flannel/cotton
9) **V-neck sweater:** lambswool/cotton knit
10) **Turtleneck shirt/scoop-neck shirt**
11) **Blazer:** velvet or tweed/linen
12) **Vest or cardigan/T-shirt or tank top** to combine with shirts

You'll see that there are more tops than bottoms on my list. That's because it's easier and less expensive to vary shirts and sweaters with just a few pairs of pants or skirts. I also like having a variety of shirts because they can be worn year-round: layered with sweaters and jackets or vests and sweater-coats in the winter and teamed with a pretty, brightly colored T-shirt in the summer. (For a special summer fashion look, you can tie a lightweight sweater around your shoulders with the tee and shirt layering.) Shirts and sweaters add color and texture to your wardrobe.

TEXTURED FABRICS

I've given you only one choice for each season's fabric. There are many, many others you might like better. Even if you're going steady with denim jeans, you'll love the feeling of these: in winter—corduroy, gabardine, wool challis, wool blends, flannel, velvet, tweed, mohair, cashmere; in summer—cotton gauze, jersey, polyester crepe de chine (a man-made silky fabric), silk, madras, cotton blends. You can combine textures to make different outfits or repeat the twelve basic pieces in as many separate fabrics as you can afford.

COLOR

My wardrobe has a lot of soft, neutral colors; they mix well with each other. Plaids and stripes don't; save them for shirts. Choose solid colors for pants and skirts. That way you can wear them with all your tops. My favorite colors are brown, beige, peach, gray, cream, teal, and black.

Pick three colors that you really like and that harmonize with each other. Two should be neutral and the third a more vibrant color. (Example: navy and cream plus yellow). When the colors can be mixed and matched, you have the key to extending a small wardrobe. And that's important when you have to make outfits for school, a part-time job, a movie date, a dinner date, a sporting event, church and holiday celebrations.

To help show you how to combine the twelve articles for dozens of looks, I've worked out a chart that lists them and teams them, with hints of what activities suit which outfit best. Since school is such an important part of your life, the clothing examples I've chosen are in fall fabrics, and most combinations are geared for classroom days. Use it as a guide, choosing your own colors and fabrics. See how many different combinations you can think of that I haven't!

Three Dozen Looks from One Dozen Fashion Selections!

	(A) Shirt-jacket (tan corduroy)	(B) Floral-print Blouson (navy, beige/navy, yellow, and tan)	(C) Tailored Shirt (beige/navy narrow stripes)	(D) V-neck Sweater (navy chenille)	(E) Turtleneck (beige lambswool)	(F) Blazer (navy velvet)	(G) Vest or Cardigan (cream, soft knit)
Pants (tan wool blend)	with (C) and vest or (E): 2 outfits for school or skating	with a solid shawl, for a date at a nice restaurant or a movie	layer these two for school, work, or a casual date at the movies or an activity like bowling	a very sophisticated look with simple gold jewelry: a chain and stud earrings; this sweater's a little too dressy; but with a simple V-neck, add (C) or (E)	a very classy look for school or Saturday afternoon shopping	a suit for an important meeting or dress up with (C); movie date	great over any shirt to give it a casual look
Pants (navy velvet, to match blazer)	no match	for a very festive occasion: a party, holiday celebration	with (F) + (G): stadium date	with a floral shawl: movie date	with (C) belted over it	to give a casual look when worn with (C); movie date	for a movie date if you add (D) to keep it from being too casual
Pants (tan corduroy, to match shirt-jacket)	perfect set! a long walk, a picnic; for school if layered with (E)	no match (the blouson's probably too dressy for casual pants)	fine for sport but add (D) to keep it from being too casual	this sweater's a very casual: for a sports event, add (F) + (G)	great with (F) for a concert	see (E) and (C)	if bulky, the look will be too sporty; if not, O.K.
Skirt (beige challis)	a very casual match for school, work, movie date	dressy for a special dinner date or dance	good for school if teamed with (D); dates, too	very dressy if worn without (C) for romantic or holiday parties	great for school or a casual lunch or shopping; add a bright scarf	add to (E) for a classy look	add this to (C) + (F)
Skirt (gray/tan tweed)	no match	no match if the blouson is too frilly	perfect for school; add (F) for more flair	too dressy to wear with this skirt	great for school or afternoon outings; add (F) for more polish	see (C) and (E)	add this to (C) + (F)

To Complete Your Wardrobe

Once you've gotten the basic components, you'll want to think about enlarging your wardrobe. But before you give up good sense for an impulsive dress buy, consider adding shirts, sweaters, pants, and skirts because of their versatility. When you are ready to buy dressier clothes, buy those that can be accented in many ways. Here are some ideas:

A DRESS

There are some special occasions when you'll want to wear a dress—to church, a dance, or a party. It's nice to have at least one good dress, but it's not as versatile as a skirt or a sweater because you can't wear it too many different ways. Choose a simple crepe de chine or jersey shirtwaist dress in a solid color. Combined with a blazer, it's a casual look; a fringed shawl will dress it up.

AN EVENING OUTFIT

It's a very special and important purchase, that first full-length dress, but it can be impractical; after all, how often do you wear it? A simple skirt that falls at mid-calf length worn with a lacy top and strappy shoes will give you the dramatic look you want. On more casual occasions, this length skirt goes well with boots and a layered-look top.

ACCESSORIES

When worn with a dress, accessories create a special look. With separates, they tie the look together. Look again at the chart. You can see how many times an accessory defines an outfit: a scarf here, a shawl there, a hint of jewelry, a belt.

Accessories add color to a neutral wardrobe, but even more importantly, they add flair, a touch of class. If you have three different scarves and wear each with the same white shirt, it'll seem as though you have three different shirts. Other accessories, like shoes and a purse, complete an outfit and work best if

153

they're in the same color family as the darkest clothes you're wearing. If you were to choose clothes in the colors suggested on the chart, navy would be the best choice. It goes with the navy clothes, of course, but also with those in yellow, tan, and beige, the other colors in the outfit. Tan-colored shoes would match some of the clothes but wouldn't look right with the navy pants. If you have two choices, it would be a good second. But with only one pair of shoes allowed, navy would complement everything.

Here's an idea of the fashion accessories you'll want to have: (★) means it adds dash; (☆) means it completes the outfit.

☆ *Shoes:* loafers or moccasins with small stacked heels for casual pants; running sneakers for jeans; simple pumps to wear with a dress; chic strappy sandals for dress-up occasions

☆ *Boots:* waterproof kind for snow and rain; dressier boots for cold dry weather or for a special indoors look

☆ *Bags:* a roomy shoulder bag for day; a canvas tote for your school books; an evening purse or clutch

☆ *Gloves:* warm knitted gloves or mittens for winter; lightweight driving gloves for cool spring or autumn weather

☆ *Hat:* knitted cap or beret for winter (to coordinate with your coat or lined raincoat); sporty straw or denim hat for summer

★ *Jewelry:* simple gold pieces (see chapter 5) or costume jewelry for around your neck; a few colored bangles for your wrists; simple earrings; a sporty watch

★ *Shawl:* one in a complementary solid color, a second in a print that includes the basic solid colors of your wardrobe

★ *Scarves:* solid squares to tie around your neck as accents; long rectangles to tie around your waist; large patterned squares for a bolder fashion statement

★ *Belts:* a simple gold-colored belt to wear with shirts over pants; a thin leather belt for a more casual look (nice with jeans); a double-wrap belt to wear over blouson tops or pretty T-shirts

Don't worry about getting everything at once. The fun of accessories is building your collection one piece at a time. Like your other clothes, the best ones are the traditional items that never go out of style (those listed above). But it's also fun to buy one trendy accessory every now and then, like a pouch bag (and it makes more sense than buying an expensive trendy *fashion* like a dress), but until you have a good-sized collection of the more classic ones (like beautiful cotton squares) browse, but don't buy.

A WINTER COAT

This is your most sensible purchase: a basic black, navy, or tan coat that covers your skirts or dresses and is keyed to the rest of your wardrobe. A belted wrap coat or a single- or double-breasted style is the traditional choice and, if you can't buy a sporty jacket too, will look right with pants as well.

To combine a winter coat and a raincoat, a pile-lined storm coat in poplin will keep you warm in the winter and, with the lining removed, dry in rainy weather.

If you can afford a sporty jacket, make it a parka-type one, in a bright color, for very cold weather or a quilted one for cool (not freezing) climates.

AND UNDER IT ALL . . .

The clothes you wear underneath those everyone sees are just as important, for two reasons: They give your body extra warmth, and they make your clothes look better. There's nothing more uncomfortable than a skirt that clings to your hose—wearing a slip will stop all that static. And wearing undergarments that add a little control to your figure will smooth the lumps and bumps even a slim girl sometimes has. With the beautiful fabrics and colors of today's lingerie, you can have a pretty undercover wardrobe, too.

Bras, hose, slips, panties, and control garments are all found in the foundation department of your favorite store. (It's called that because these clothes are the foundation to all those you put on afterwards, just like a makeup foundation is the base for all other makeup.) The saleswomen in this area, unlike those in other departments, are specially trained to fit you—like a *corsetière* when corsets were the thing. (Fortunately for us, the garment industry found a replacement for whalebone in bras!) Some items, like slips, are sized according to your waist measurement, but others, like panties, have a different system (sizes

4 to 8) that has nothing to do with skirt or pants size. The foundation fitter will be able to use your measurements to find the right sizes for you. Here's what you should know before you shop.

Your bust (measure just *under* the bosom for your bra size, then
> measure at the fullest part to calculate your cup size: If one inch wider, your cup size is "A." If two inches wider, "B"; three inches wider, "C," and so on. So if a girl measures 34 inches below her bosom, and 36 inches at the fullest part, her bra size is 34B.

Your waist (measured at the narrowest part)
Your hips (measure at the hipbone)

You'll find a mind-boggling selection, especially at the bra counter (the most important one you'll shop at). To clear up some of the confusion:

Bras. This is the most important foundation you'll ever need. Physically, you need the support it gives—without a bra, a girl with a large bust can suffer with backaches and hunched shoulders from the unsupported weight—and, from an aesthetic point of view, you need the shapely look it provides. I've seen too many girls who have abandoned wearing a bra and I don't think that's a good idea at all. A bra is a useful garment—without it, the delicate tissues of the breasts can weaken and stretch and eventually begin to sag.

Bras are made in many different styles, but the element that separates them is not really the color of the fabric or whether or not it has lace trim. It's the support each style gives you. Of course the amount of support you need depends on the size of your bust. Bras come in different cup sizes, from AAA (the smallest) to A to D to DDD (the biggest). And the larger your cup size, the more support you need from the construction of the bra. Unfortunately, the cute little bra and panty sets that usually say "one size fits all" are the worst kind for girls who have begun to develop. Sure they're cute, but if they aren't going to do a thing for your figure, who needs them?

Support in a bra comes from the construction underneath the cups, not from pulling the straps tight (this can leave permanent dents in your shoulders). Girls who need support need *underwire* bras (a thin wire is worked underneath the folds of fabric to mold the bra cups to your size) with a wider back (three hooks instead of just one or two).

Front-closing bras are attractive and some have underwire construction, but they generally don't give as much support as those that close in back.

Totally *unconstructed* bras (the kind that come in a set with panties) are fine for girls with an A cup or smaller. Even if they do come in a larger cup size, they will only cover over; they won't lift and support.

When choosing a bra, look for those that enable you to change the elastic straps. The elastic often runs out of stretch before you need to buy a new bra. Slipping in new ones will increase the durability of the foundation.

If you wear a lot of knit shirts and sweaters, you'll want a smooth-cupped bra made in a nylon fabric, rather than a lacy one whose outline could show through your top (wear this one with woven shirts). If you have an outfit with spaghetti straps, you'll want to get a strapless bra. This one definitely needs underwire construction and maybe four or five hooks to hold it around your torso. Flimsy tube-shaped bras won't do any good.

You should have three or more bras so that you can alternate them. Even if you wash it every night, wearing the same bra each day will wear it out quickly. You can have the same style in each bra, if you like the look and it gives you the support you need. Choose bras in neutral shades like flesh or beige; you should have one in white, too, and if you wear lots of navy or black or dark brown, have one in any of these colors, also. Many well-constructed bras are part of matched sets, too, some with lace accents.

Slips. To stop fabric from clinging to your tights or pantyhose, wearing a slip is a must. Also, when worn under lightweight skirts or dresses, it will stop light from giving everyone around you "X-ray vision." A slip will also help smooth a fabric that clings to your little bulges.

Slips are made in two basic styles: the full slip and the half slip. The first goes on over your head and covers from your shoulders to your knees. The second goes only from your waist to your knees, where it is most needed (more comfortable than the full version).

You can choose a full-skirt half-slip or a straighter, narrower one, depending on the cut of the skirt you'll be wearing with it. For most clothes, choose one in beige. A white one works well under most colors, but for navy, browns, or black skirts, you'll want a very dark one, too. You need only one light and one dark in your wardrobe.

Aside from the waist measurement, which determines the basic size, you'll need a hip measurement if your hips are more than 10 inches wider than your waist and a fuller-style half or full slip.

Also important is the length of the slip from the waist to the hem. It varies from 20 to 30 or more inches. Measure your dresses and skirts and take the *shortest* measurement for your first slip. (If it falls 3 or so inches shorter than your longest skirt, it won't really matter, but 3 inches longer than your shortest skirt will have you pulling it up constantly and wondering whether it's sticking out!)

Panties. When you're buying these in the junior department, the various brands will give you a size chart, on the back of the package, to let you figure out your size. In the foundations department, panties run in set sizes or small, medium, or large. The saleswoman will know how to find your proper size, using your hip measurement. You can try them on, over your own panties, to be sure. (Because manufacturers use fabrics that stretch easily, it's hard to say that every size 5, for instance, will be the same; some run large, others small.)

The underpants should fit comfortably at the thighs and hips, or waist, if you prefer briefs to bikini-style. They shouldn't make a bulge or indentation at the band. If they do, they're too small. Those with cotton panels or all-cotton ones are better than nylon ones because they let your skin "breathe." You should have eight or more pairs.

Pantyhose or tights. With the discovery of pantyhose, girls said goodbye to awkward garter belts and stockings. Pantyhose are usually worn over your underpants, but sometimes that creates bulges. Today, you can buy panties and pantyhose in one.

Choose sandalfoot hose when wearing sandals or open toe or heel shoes; they don't have the reinforced fabric on these areas. For shoes and boots, it makes sense to wear the kind with reinforcement; they protect the easily ripped parts of the hose. Buy pantyhose as you need them, but keep a pair or two of extras in case of unforeseen rips. To help preserve your hose, be sure that your nails are well filed before you put them on; a jagged edge will cause a rip. Remove all rings and bracelets that can catch on the hose, too. Sit down to put them on; this is no time to be hopping around on one foot! Gather each leg at the toe and slip it over one foot, then the other. Shifting from left to right and back, ease the hose up your legs little by little. Raise your hips to slide the pantyhose over them and adjust the waistband. Do small knee bends to be sure you can move easily and check to see that the seams, if any, are straight. Follow the suggestions in chapter 14 for their care.

Control garments. Control panties, all-in-ones, and long-leg girdles all control bulges with heavy stretch fabrics. I don't think you should come to depend on them because after a short time, they can cause ridges and marks and slow your circulation, if worn every day. But until diet and exercise put you in shape, you can rely on one of these to tighten up flab temporarily, but they won't work any disappearing acts:

A *control panty* is a waist-high pair of underpants that firms and flattens your stomach and rear. It's made of a lightweight stretch fabric and doesn't have any heavy panels.

An *all-in-one* is a control panty plus a long-line bra combined in a leotardlike foundation for one smooth line. You can get one with or without heavy control panels and with or without the long-leg bottom.

A *long-leg girdle* or panty is the longer version that tightens the thighs as well as the hips and stomach. It gives you a sleeker line, especially if you have heavy thighs. (A panty girdle makes your thighs seem extra large because it tightens your hips.)

Just for fun. Tap pants and camisoles and teddys have come back (from the 1940s) in silkly fabrics with lacy trims. These are fun to wear instead of a nightgown, but unless you can do without the support of a bra, they are out for wearing as underwear. You can wear a teddy over your bra, but it won't give you the benefits of a slip, and it can feel too bulky. Still, it can make going to sleep special.

159

To get the most out of your underwear, be sure that each piece is properly fitted, for comfort and looks. Though you're the only one who knows they're there, they can, if properly chosen, do as much for your fashion savvy as your "real" clothes.

12.

Fashion Savvy: Wardrobe Illusions

JUST AS WITH makeup and perfume and all the other beauty steps you take, your clothes should flatter you. Sounds simple, doesn't it? But it isn't always the case. How many times have you bought a skirt or a sweater because of its pretty color or its style or because it was "in"? When wearing it, how many times have you said to yourself, There's something that's just not right about it. That "something" is the skirt or the sweater itself. The pretty color and the fashion styling don't matter if the garment doesn't fit and flatter *you*.

If it looks great on the hanger but not so great on you, put it back, even if it's what you're "always wanted." That's a fashion rule every girl can follow. And it's a must for girls who depend on the fashions they buy to work a little magic on their figure.

It doesn't matter if you're thin or heavy, the clothes you buy and wear have to be tapered to your size. Even though I'm thin now, I can wind up looking twenty pounds heavier if I wear the wrong kind of clothes. Once you know the styles and cuts that look good on your shape—and those that don't—you can save a lot of shopping time and a lot of wasted money. (You hardly ever wear clothes that don't look right; they sit in the closet, collecting dust until you admit your mistake and give them away.)

Wardrobe illusions are created by buying clothes that camouflage your size. Unlike foundations, which redistribute and smooth your bulges, these clothes only give an illusion. If you're overweight, you can combine both methods for greater success.

Because our bodies are all unique, our problem areas vary. You may have one or more of these trouble spots. Follow all the suggestions that apply to your shape.

161

Trouble Spots

IF YOU'RE OVERWEIGHT, and waiting for the results of a diet to show, there are some general rules to follow:

1. Avoid prints, especially when choosing pants and skirts. They seem to spell F–A–T.

2. Avoid heavy, bulky fabrics or knits, like cable-stitch sweaters and tweeds. Tight-fitting, clingy fabrics accentuate bulges, too. Choose crisp fabrics that hold their shape.

3. Use the same light and dark technique you use with makeup: Wear light colors on your best figure features, dark ones to camouflage and minimize the bulges.

4. Vertical stripes minimize; horizontal stripes accentuate. It's always better to choose solid colors and add a printed or striped scarf as an accent.

5. Camouflage with loose clothing. Tight clothes always look tight—and can make you look like a sausage.

Now for the specifics:

IF YOU HAVE BROAD HIPS, minimize them with skirts and dresses cut in an A-line—narrow at the waist, gathering fullness toward the hem like the widening sides of the letter "A."

Coordinate your tops and bottoms: A matched skirt and blouse or pants and a sweater give you a sleek line, especially when all are in solid blue, black, brown, or gray. If you wear a skirt and top, be sure that your hose and shoes are in the same color. This too will give a long, slim-line look because there's no contrast between your hemline, your legs, and your feet.

When you're wearing pants, choose tunic-length tops that fall in an A-line as well, gathering fullness from the bust to the bottom. Full smock shirts and peasant blouses are also good.

Don't wear little bolero-type jackets or vests that cut the sleek line. Sweaters that end at the waist do the same. Wear sweater-coats instead.

IF YOU HAVE A THICK WAISTLINE, wear narrow-leg pants with the same style tunic tops to hide the tummy roll. Vests that fall in a straight line to the hips are very flattering over blouses.

Smock dresses worn over a pretty turtleneck will look fashionable and be slimming, too.

Blouson tops that are gathered at the hips can be worn on dressier occasions. Avoid waist-length sweaters that cut your figure in two. These also apply if you are SHORT-WAISTED.

IF YOU HAVE HEAVY LEGS, wear full skirts and interesting tops to shift attention upward. The skirts should be a longer, mid-calf length. Team them with boots when weather permits (the skirt should cover the top of the boots) for a longer line.

When you must wear pants, choose those that flare from the thigh, not from the knee. To keep the cuffs from swatting each other, tuck them into boots or roll them at mid-calf over the boots.

Always stay away from jersey and nylon fabrics that cling to bulges.

IF YOU ARE BOWLEGGED, you can wear skirts if you choose full ones, like a dirndl or a pleated kilt (avoid pleats if you're broad in the hips).

Avoid knee-length, narrow skirts that draw attention to your legs.

IF YOU HAVE SHORT LEGS AND A LONG TORSO, wear dresses with a raised waistline, like Empire-style ones. Short vests and bolero jackets are good, too.

IF YOUR UPPER ARMS ARE LARGE OR FLABBY, start exercising right away. Until you tone these muscles, don't wear sleeveless or strapless blouses or dresses.

In summer, wear cotton shirts with smocked three-quarter sleeves, or knit tops with sleeves that can be pushed up, or T-shirts with bell sleeves.

Dolman-sleeved sweaters and blousons are great in cooler weather.

IF YOU HAVE A LARGE BUST, minimize it by teaming dark-colored blouses with light-colored slacks and skirts (if you're thin through the middle). If you wear a light skirt, combine it with a darker or a print sweater.

Avoid shirts with breast pockets and don't wear clingy sweaters that only accentuate your chest.

IF YOU HAVE A SMALL BUST, reverse the above ideas!
Try wearing sweaters with interesting necklines, like a cowl-neck sweater or a boat-neck pullover.

IF YOU HAVE ROUNDED SHOULDERS, wear a blazer with a little padding over your blouses.
Shirts with bell sleeves and yoked shoulders add fullness, too. Stay away from revealing knits.

IF YOU HAVE A LONG NECK, wear high collars, like turtlenecks and cowl-neck sweaters.

IF YOU HAVE A SHORT NECK, wear V-neck and sweetheart necklines to add the illusion of a higher neck.

IF YOU'RE TOO THIN, you can wear fashionable knit sweaters, layered on top of shirts and turtlenecks without worrying about looking large. Team them with straight-leg pants (you can wear those with pleats, too!).
If the layered look is too overpowering because of a small bone structure, like mine, wear full skirts and a blouson top to add fullness without bulkiness. Bright colors, shiny fabrics, and horizontal stripes do the same.

IF YOU'RE SHORT, combine the sleekness of a straight skirt, hemmed just under the knee, with a tailored blouse to give you a slimmer, taller-looking silhouette.
If you like to wear pants but find that they are too baggy or the seat is too low, ask your tailor to taper them to fit you. (The department store or boutique might have a tailor on the premises.)
Outfits all in one color add dimension, too; find a matching sweater or blouse to wear with those pants.
Wear accessories, but don't let an overlong scarf or a huge shoulder bag overpower you!

IF YOU'RE TALL, don't give up wearing higher heels. Instead, establish a contrast by wearing a bright-colored blouse with a deeper-colored pair of pants or a skirt.

You can get away with a look that is difficult for most girls: straight-leg pants with a smock blouse, topped by a sporty vest. That kind of layering cuts your figure in a way that reduces your height.

Your accessories can be large and bold.

FOR EVERY GIRL: The best fashion advice is to buy the right size for you and be sure everything fits properly. It's silly to buy a size 9 when you know that your hips are a size 13, even if you can get the zipper up. If it upsets you to buy that larger size, cut off the size tags as soon as you get home; no one will know but you. And the clothing will fit. Don't make the mistake of buying a size smaller than the one you need, even if the item's on sale. Even when you do lose your extra pounds, you won't be guaranteed that it will fit—your bones are something you can't change, and you'll have a piece of clothing that's not wearable. Buy a pair of pants in the size you wear *when you buy them*. When you lose weight, you can have them taken in. That's one way to keep your clothes for a long period of time; the other is . . . to sew them yourself!

13.

Fashion Savvy: Sew It Yourself

THERE'S A LOT more to sewing than replacing a button on a shirt! Knowing how to sew has enabled me to keep fashions that are more than five years old. As my body changed —I lost weight, I grew a few inches—I was able to alter my pants and skirts. If you know how to use a needle and thread or a sewing machine, you don't ever have to worry about fluctuating hemlines. If you want to listen to fashion orders each season, you can simply adjust your clothes.

I learned how to sew from my mother—after having seven of her eight sons, she could hardly stop sewing clothes for me. It's a craft I'll pass on to my daughters, too.

With clothes' prices being as crazy as they are—and sure to get even higher—being able to sew means being able to build a wardrobe without much money. You can use patterns by any of the fashion design studios, or you can even select a designer outfit from your favorite magazine, adapt it to your own proportions, and sew it for a fraction of the cost. With ready-made fashions being so expensive, it's no wonder that sewing is making a comeback.

Once you feel comfortable behind the sewing machine, there's no reason why you shouldn't try your hand at designing, too. It seemed like a very natural thing for me. I started working with the Butterick pattern people only a couple of years ago— and not just modeling. The fashions I model for patterns are fashions that I've helped design. I have definite opinions on style, fabric, and design, as well as my own sewing sense. I like those that are easy to sew and easy to wear. All the styles that bear my name are ones that I would and do wear and feel comfortable in. I think they're appropriate for my age group and for a teen's lifestyle. If I was shown a design that I didn't like, Butterick and I would work together to alter it, to suit both you and

*At first tackling a new project
can be difficult . . .*

*. . . but soon it becomes an
absorbing and rewarding
challenge.*

167

me. It's fun for me to be involved in designing because I've always loved fashion.

Fortunately, my family has given me lots of opportunities to express my ideas. I've designed costumes for the Osmond Brothers' television specials—and even had a credit at the end of the show! It's nice to have time to be creative, but my brothers gave me a two-week deadline. I found that you can't cut corners when you have only a few days to bring to life pictures on a piece of paper. (The designs were flown to Los Angeles where professional tailors went to work on them.) Since then we've gone to work on a whole line of clothes, named Olive's Kids, for my mother and her nine children, of course! Both Mother and I have contributed to the design of the clothes, which are all moderately priced and available for guys and girls. See where a little sewing can lead?

How to start: Take a sewing class at a sewing center, a "Y" or a crafts' school. If you have trouble finding one near you, call a local fabric store and ask for their suggestions.

If your mother knows how to sew, ask her to teach you. If you don't have a sewing machine, ask to borrow a friend's or visit an appliance store and find out about renting one while you learn.

Marie's Special Hints for Sewing Savvy

1. When you finish sewing a seam, press it down right away. It will give the garment the professional finish you see on store-bought clothes.

2. Always adjust a pattern to the kind of fabric you'll be using. If you're working with a light, sheer fabric like silk, you'll probably want to eliminate unnecessary pockets and stitching that can show through. If you use a heavier fabric, like a denim, you can add a zipper or buttons to a basic pattern—or even top-stitching to turn any pants design into "jeans."

3. When you're going to be working with a new stitch, experiment with it on a scrap of the fabric you'll be using. Even if you've used the stitch before, it could give a totally different effect on another kind of fabric.

4. It does take extra time, but for major pieces, consider lining the garment. It increases its durability and helps the gar-

ment hang smoothly, without the need for a slip. It sounds extravagant, but lining pants really makes them wear beautifully, and makes you feel great. Lining also makes it possible to use fabrics that would be too rough or itchy against your skin but which have a nice look to them. The color of the lining should match the predominant color of the clothing fabric and have compatible care instructions. (Don't line a fabric that has to be dry cleaned with one that must be hand washed!)

5. Know all your measurements before you select a pattern, not just your waist but hips, too, for pants and skirts. And remember that it's easier to adjust a waist measurement than one for your hips. If you have figure problems, look for the styles recommended for your shape in chapter 12.

Sewing is only one of the beautiful crafts you can learn. There are many others that are as much fun and can give your wardrobe a boost. If any of these interests you, investigate it in the crafts section of your library. These can all be self-taught with a book and a minimum of tools:

- Knitting: sweaters, scarves, hats, mittens, mufflers
- Crocheting: pullover tops, disco pouches, hats, belts
- Macrame: jewelry, vests, hair ornaments
- Embroidery: decorating jeans, shirts, scarves
- Batik: a process that lets you design unique patterns on fabric
- Weaving: sweaters, capes, shawls, scarves

14.

Fashion Savvy: Clothes Care

IF YOU TAKE special care of your clothes, they'll last longer. At home, I do my own wardrobe upkeep. It's easy once you get organized. And it's necessary if you want to look your best. I've organized all the clothes care know-how I've learned in these tips.

Organization

The key to keeping your wardrobe in order is organization. Everything has a place and every place has a thing: Know what goes where. Label storage boxes in detail so that you know where your favorite red sweater is without having to search every corner.

- SEPARATE your shirts from your sweaters in your drawers. Unless one shirt only goes with one particular sweater, clothes should be organized by family . . . in your closet too: Skirts, Pants, Vests, etc. That way you'll never have to worry about missing relatives!
- DIVIDE your lingerie drawers into compartments for bras, panties, pantyhose. Most chests come with two or four top drawers, half the size of those beneath. These are for the smaller items in your wardrobe (belts and scarves too). If your dresser drawers are all the same size, divide them with cardboard squares standing upright, as for your lingerie. Or paper each section in a different color to mark the divisions.
- CHOOSE different-colored hangers for dresses, skirts, and pants. If these garments intermingle, you can always spot what you want by glancing at the hangers.

- CHOOSE the right kind of hanger for each type of garment: hangers with clips for skirts, lightly padded hangers for dresses and sweater coats or vests, wooden hangers for pants (to keep them from creasing), heavily padded hangers for coats, a five-branch hanger for blouses, skirts, and pants (five hangers attached to one pole for accommodating five items in the space of one). Wire hangers that come from the cleaners aren't sturdy and promote wrinkles. Recycle them by transferring clothes to your own hangers and return the wire ones to the cleaners.
- SAVE the boxes shoes come in. They protect your shoes from dust and can be stacked one on top of the other. Label each box so that you can find the pair you want easily. (You can even cover the box with paper to match your hangers: If green is for pants, cover your casual shoes' box with the same color paper.)
- SAVE space, if your closet is small, by using a shoe bag holder on your closet door. The cloth pouches protect shoes and take up less room than the boxes.
- CONVERT a single clothes rod to accommodate more garments if you don't need the shelf above. This shelf can be removed and the existing rack raised closer to the ceiling. A second rack, for shirts and skirts, can be added just below where the first one used to be.

Wardrobe Upkeep

- PROTECT purses by stuffing them with tissue paper when they are not being used. This helps them hold their shape.
- FRESHEN shoes with a spray of cologne. Sprinkle baby powder on the insole before you put them on, to absorb odors during the day.
- NEATNESS counts when you're laundering your clothes, too. Organize clothes into piles: hand wash, machine wash, dry clean, launder professionally.
- KEEP clothes fresher longer by hanging them up as soon as you take them off, if they don't need to be laundered.
- DON'T put soiled clothes back into the closet after you've worn them; if you reach for something to wear and find it soiled,

don't throw it to the bottom of your closet. Care for your clothes as they need it.

- SET aside one afternoon or evening (only a couple of hours) each weekend to plan what you'll wear the following week and to check all the clothes for repairs or laundering needs. If you've been collecting a pile of clothes that need to be hand washed, do them now. Or catch up with your sewing: Check for loose buttons or labels, gapping hemlines and ripped linings.
- IF the care instructions on a new outfit are printed on a separate card rather than on the garment label, carefully remove the card and mark it immediately with a description of the outfit. Place the card in your sewing box for future reference. You can ruin an outfit by cleaning it the wrong way.
- ALWAYS have one emergency outfit ready, in case the dress you were planning to wear isn't delivered in time from the cleaners or if your little sister spills her apple juice on you as you kiss her goodbye on your way to school.
- KEEP a pretty box filled with your repair and care tools: threads and needles, extra buttons that came with outfits, shoe polish, a clothes brush for removing lint or even your pet's hairs.
- POLISH shoes and your purse if needed the night before you plan to wear them. You may not have time in the morning.
- DRY CLEANERS are notorious for losing belts and bows. If a belt doesn't need cleaning, but the outfit it belongs to does, keep it at home. If the belt does need to be dry cleaned, point it out to the person who writes out the stub and have it clearly printed.
- BE SURE you can easily read a description of every item you bring to the cleaners, for you protection and theirs. Don't rely on memory—theirs or yours. If the clerk's handwriting isn't legible to you, write the items in yourself and have him or her initial each.
- POINT OUT difficult spots or stains on garments that you take to the cleaners. They may have a special solution to remove it.
- HAND WASH all delicate fabrics with a special cold water wash product. Fill your basin with cool water, add a capful of the product, swoosh the garments in the sudsy water, and let them soak for five minutes. Rinse with lots of cool water and blot dry in a terry towel. Hang them to dry. This is the best way to

wash: pantyhose, bras, control garments. Usually they don't need ironing.

- MACHINE WASH permanent press shirts, skirts, and pants that you feel you can iron yourself (there are usually two or three wrinkles). But if it says "Dry clean only," believe it. . . . even if it looks like you can do the job yourself.
- SWEATERS that are labeled "hand wash" should be washed in a cold water sudsing product. Rinse in cold water after soaking and wrap it up in a terry towel to remove excess water (squeezing or stretching wool when wet will ruin its shape). Now lie it flat on a dry towel and smooth it out. Let it dry naturally. If somehow a sweater gets into the washing machine, get it out before it gets into the dryer. Rinse it in cold water and put it on wet to get it back to its normal state (you might have to stretch it a little). Once it gives, take it off and block it out on a towel to dry. *Note:* If this doesn't work, chalk it up to experience and be more careful next time.
- JEANS tend to shrink in the washer and dryer, even at cold and cool cycles. If you can't afford to have them shrink at all, consider sending them to the dry cleaners.
- BLOUSES and SHIRTS will look spanking brand new if they're professionally laundered every now and then for a crisp finish. If you wear them as overblouses, not tucked into pants or a skirt, have them placed on hangers, not boxed or folded which sets in wrinkles.
- ALWAYS follow manufacturers' directions for the care and laundering of clothes. Read the labels before you buy to see if you can afford the upkeep: Too many clothes that need to be dry cleaned can take a big dent out of your allowance, even if they are nicer than those you can just toss into the washing machine. If you buy clothes that need to be hand washed, remember to set aside an hour every few days and an afternoon once every week. (Pantyhose and bras will need to be washed more frequently than a blouse you wear only once a week.)

Add these tips together and your clothes will have the look of good grooming—the difference between just having the right clothes and really looking stunning in them.

15.
Memo from Marie: Fashion from High School to College

IT'S HARD TO say when you really feel grown up. Nothing all that dramatic happens the day after a birthday. But there's no feeling more magical or special than the one you get on your first day of college. It doesn't matter if you attend your hometown university or if you go away from home—something happens as you cross that invisible border and go from "childhood" to the "adult world" (or so it seems!). All of a sudden, you're ready to throw away everything in your closet and start over again—adding a sophisticated touch. Though the funny thing about college is that, if anything, clothing styles are more relaxed. Everyone is trying to get away from the uniform of high school and fashion seems to go wild. Army surplus, disco dresses, jeans-and-T-shirt combinations intermingle, and good fashion sense is lost in all the hoopla.

At some college campuses, sweater sets and A-line skirts make up the preferred outfit; at others, anything but jeans is out! It always helps to visit the school in the spring of the year you'll be attending to see what trends are favored. These are only some of the most frequently seen "looks" in college catalog photos: white painter's pants worn with a turtleneck sweater and clogs; Armylike olive drab jeans with a matching olive shirt and cardigan; straight-leg pants, stacked-heel loafers, a print shirt and blazer; the unconstructed blazer with push-up sleeves worn over everything; a soft blouson sweater worn over a pleated skirt; Western boots with everything.

If you have trouble finding out which style is really you, I'd like to suggest thirty different ensembles—complete with accessories. You'll see that many include pieces from the "basic 12" collection in chapter 11. New suggestions will be frequently repeated, so build your wardrobe with these.

It's often hard to make the transition from high school to college, and it helps to know you look your best. Your wardrobe can be easily updated to look casual yet classic—and more grown-up! PHOTOCRAFT

(1) Pleated mocha wool trousers, a cream-colored shawl-collar blouse in a satiny fabric, a chocolate cardigan sweater, stacked-heel loafers, a saddle bag

(2) Gray-and-white tweed blazer, yellow cowl-neck sweater, gray knife-pleated skirt, black pumps, a roomy black shoulder bag

(3) Western corduroy jeans in forest green, a plaid shirt, green-and-white tweed vest, penny loafers, a shoulder-strap tote

(4) Straight-leg jeans, a bright-colored chenille sweater and matching thin scarf, Western boots, a saddle bag

(5) Navy corduroy jacket and skirt, plaid shirt with a narrow black tie, navy pumps and bag

(6) Cable-knit sweater-jacket in cream color, Western cord jeans in forest green, loafers, saddle bag

(7) Red plaid shirt and vest with a white tie, Western jeans, Western boots, saddle bag

(8) Lambswool dress in lavender, navy double wrap belt, navy pumps and bag

(9) Elasticized-waist pants in black, cream-color Oxford-style shirt, black-and-red striped V-neck oversweater, stacked loafers, black shoulder bag

(10) Navy cord blazer, straight-leg jeans, shawl-collared blouse, navy pumps or boots and bag

(11) Wool tied-sleeve smock in teal, straight-leg corduroy pants in teal, cream turtleneck under smock, stacked loafers, saddle bag

(12) Wool smock, plaid shirt underneath, matching plaid vest over smock, black elasticized-waist pants, black loafers with low heels, roomy black tote

(13) Bright yellow jacquard tunic, rust pegged pants in wool blend, rust leather boots, saddle bag

(14) Flannel shirt in a plaid, straight-leg cord jeans in the dominant color of the plaid, a double wrap belt, tan clogs, saddle bag

(15) Challis shirt, in deep pink, over challis skirt in small pink and black print with a black double wrap belt, black pumps and bag

(16) Apricot-color blouson in velours, teal straight-leg pants, teal print scarf to tie around neck, stacked loafers, saddle bag

(17) Yellow plaid shirt with imitation mother-of-pearl snaps, solid yellow wool man's vest, navy cord skirt, navy shoes or boots and bag

(18) Gray-and-white tweed blazer, cream shawl-collared blouse, black pants, shoes, and bag

(19) Apricot velour blouson, rust pegged pants, boots, saddle bag

(20) Rust cowl-neck sweater, straight-leg jeans tucked into rust boots, saddle bag, long cashmere scarf with fringe

(21) Tweed blazer, cream turtleneck sweater, cream tweed skirt, stacked loafers, saddle bag

(22) Shiny black rain slicker, yellow cowl sweater, straight-leg cord jeans, tucked into shiny black rubber boots, a shiny black tote with shoulder straps

(23) Cream cowl sweater, green-and-white tweed vest, forest green corduroy skirt, stacked loafers, saddlebag

(24) Cable-knit sweater-jacket, straight-leg cords, penny loafers, shoulder tote

(25) Pink challis shirt, black pants, shoes, and tote

(26) Yellow jacquard tunic, yellow vest, straight-leg jeans, Western boots, saddle bag

(27) Pleated wool trousers, cream cowl sweater, topped by pink challis shirt, stacked loafers, saddle bag

(28) Yellow plaid shirt, chocolate cardigan sweater, straight-leg jeans, running sneakers, saddle bag

(29) Plaid skirt with matching shawl, tied over cream cowl sweater, black pumps and bag

(30) Gray flannel pants, yellow cowl sweater and shawl from (29), black black pumps and bag

You can keep the cominations growing with each new pair of pants or skirt you buy. It's easy once you practice, and lots of fun, knowing that you never have to worry about looking out of date . . . as long as you choose clothes that never go out of style.

PHOTOCRAFT

178

Our World . . .
and Your Place in It

In the first fifteen chapters of this book, I've shared with you all the things I've learned to enhance your natural assets. The subjects have been quite different, but all are equally important and exciting. They have one special goal in common: to make you the most attractive girl you can be. It takes a little practice to get everything working together, but once you start, you begin to see the terrific results.

When I look at pictures taken of me five or six years ago, it's hard for me to believe I'm the same girl I am today. My photographs show how much we can improve the way we look as we have the fun of applying makeup or learning a new exercise or discovering new hairstyles. But I've also found that putting beauty knowledge to work on the outside is only half the story. There's another, very important part of begin pretty: inner beauty.

We develop it by building our personality and expanding our outlook on life to include not just you and me, but a whole new universe filled with many different people. Most of us will meet only a handful of those who make up our diverse world. But this small, yet important group—our family, our friends, and those around us— are extra special; they help mold our personality. Knowing how to build a relationship with each of them is a beauty lesson, too.

179

16.
Who Am I?

THAT'S A QUESTION we all ask at different times in our life, though most often in our teens as we grow up and grow aware of the world around us and the different possibilities it offers. These years are important because they enable us to find out the answer to who we are, what we like and don't like, what we want and don't want.

Growing up is a lot like putting on makeup—it takes a lot of trial and error to get it right. This is a time for learning from our mistakes, from the examples of others—the people who are a part of our lives—and from everything around us that gives us a sense of quality.

My mother once told me the story of the "blue vase" and I'd like to share it with you.

There was an antique store that featured a beautiful blue vase in its window. Each day, a young factory worker would walk past the shop to look at it. Once, he went inside to price the vase; it was very expensive. He continued going by the shop every morning until, finally, he entered it again, this time with the money he had saved to purchase the antique. The owners of the shop could tell that he wasn't a very wealthy person, and they asked why he would spend so much of his savings in this way. He explained that he lived alone, in only one room, and that everything he surrounded himself with was of the highest quality: the paintings on the walls, the books he read, the records he listened to, the friends he cherished. The blue vase continued this ideal of quality in his life.

My mother bought a blue vase, which she keeps on the mantel in our home, to symbolize the search for quality in our lives. Always seeking this goal is what builds character and personality.

Today especially, it's pretty hard for each of us to find his or her own identity because there seem to be too many Indians and not enough Chiefs. (Adults usually say the opposite, but this isn't true when we're growing up!) Very often, especially when you're in school, girls and guys follow "the crowd" and lose their identity rather than express their own opinion. Being afraid of being laughed at or left on the outside is a real fear—no one likes to be left out. It seems easier to let the class leader decide what's right than to risk speaking up and being rejected. It's even worse if we're not close to our parents—we seek our friends' approval even more. After all, if they don't accept us, who will? We end up conforming to the group's standards, not our own. If the group smokes or takes drugs, the kids who want to be part of that group smoke or take drugs. If the group gets sexually involved, they go along, too, even though they all know the trouble that lies ahead. But even worse than that is the fact that those who follow never really get to learn about themselves. They get lost in the crowd and lose their individuality. Sure it's easy to become "sophisticated," but I think that we should try for something that's more satisfying than a temporary high. (We should have more respect for our bodies and ourselves, too.) It can be tempting to follow someone else and be assured of being accepted; it's easy to be concerned only with the present, and it's hard to say no to a persuasive friend because it's nice to have friends. But we should look to the future, too, and prepare for it by developing our individuality now. If we can persuade ourselves that our views and opinions have to be counted, too, we can persuade our friends.

If you don't like the way your crowd is going, find an alternative, even if at first you think you might lose your friends. If that's how you have to keep them, they aren't worthy of your friendship! A good friend of mine was very unhappy at her high school because of all the pressure to do what was "in" with the most popular group. She wanted to make the most of her education, but she felt uncomfortable with the choices that her "friends" were making. She had the courage to stick to her opinions and change schools; now she's enjoying teen life with a new group of friends. Of course, that was a drastic change. And if her first high school hadn't been so small, she probably could have found new friends there. The quality I most admire about her is that she never lost sight of herself, and she didn't let anyone turn her into a follower.

When girls (and guys) are talked into joining the others in a particular crowd, it's often by a very attractive classmate who is popular in all the social circles. But, if you want to, you can be a leader, too, even if you lead only yourself. You can be as important and outstanding as any girl in your class—even the one you most envy now. If you don't feel as blessed as she is, it could be because you haven't tried to make something of yourself yet. But with a little motivation and effort—the same kind I had to find in myself—you can develop your beauty and your inner assets. You already know how to start: Make yourself attractive, by learning to use makeup, by finding the right hairstyle that best flatters you (you won't even need that envied girl's blond hair!), by improving your figure if that's your problem area. Maybe you don't have all the makings of a beauty contest winner, but you probably have another talent that she doesn't have: a special way with words, a great ear for music, a creative bend toward art or dance or drama. You don't have to be famous or the prettiest or the best dressed or the best anything to be special, to be a somebody, as long as you make the most of what you have.

When I first felt that I wanted to improve myself, I sat down and made a list of my strong points and my weak ones. I made another list: how to improve my strong points to make up for weak ones that can't be changed (like a facial feature or your bone structure). You can make a plain face into a pretty one with makeup; you can clear bad skin by improving skin-care habits or seeing a dermatologist; you can play up your eyes to detract from a big nose. The one thing I tried never to do was get depressed or blue about myself—that won't accomplish anything, I found out! The one thing I always did and still do is to try to look my best at all times; it's a head start to putting your best foot forward and getting your point across. People pay attention to a girl who looks as smart as she sounds. (If you want advice about a special beauty problem, like skin care or weight reduction, turn back to the Table of Contents and find the specific chapter you need.)

After I worked on the outside, I began to develop the inner me. I think that education is probably the best thing a girl can have going for her. Knowledge makes us interesting to others and can help us find our own way. One reason that we teens are unsure of who we are is that we're just starting out and finding that there are so many different directions to go in that our heads spin! Making ourselves special begins with making the most of our education—it helps us learn to know what is right and what isn't, for each of us.

High school is an experience that we all go through—like it or not. It can be fun, cliquey, painful, and sometimes, it is all of these! It's hard to appreciate school if we'd rather be at the movies or listening to music—and it's impossible to understand why parents talk about their school years as "the good ole days." Dull teachers don't help much either. But I found that if you look for ways of making class interesting, it will go more smoothly. Think of History like makeup—sounds funny, doesn't it? If you tell yourself that your looks are hopeless, you'll get an "F" in the beauty department. But if you say, Hey, all the different things I can do with my eyes is fantastic, you'll graduate with honors. If you tell yourself that History is a drag, your grades will prove it. But if you do the reading and find something exciting to investigate—like the fashions of the period or the history of makeup and perfumes that were used (and date all the way back to Cleopatra), you'll get yourself interested and you'll have something to add to the class discussion, instead of couching down in your chair, hoping that your teacher doesn't notice you. Literature, the arts, history, geography—all these disciplines open the world to you, get you interested and make you interesting.

You're probably thinking that this will work for some subjects, but what about—Math, for instance. I spent many months wondering when I would ever need to use long division! And then I realized how often we call on our basic knowledge of numbers —from keeping our allowance budgets balanced to helping with family finances. Home Economics class will really help later on when you have a family—this subject is another one of life's basics that we think we'll never need, until we realize that we use many of the tools it teaches in everyday life.

Sure, high school means parties, dates, and dances, even meeting new friends, but it can mean so much more if you care enough about yourself to want to be special. If you aren't planning on going to college to study for a specialized career, it's important to learn all you can in high school. And if you are going to college, high school is an invaluable aid in preparing you for new responsibilities.

College is a different kind of challenge, one that I enjoy. Because of performing, I'm not able to attend full-time, so I take courses when I can. If earning a living is or will be keeping you from going, you might consider auditing courses on the weekends or evenings. (Auditing means that you attend the classes and do the work, but you aren't graded and don't receive credit toward a degree.) I think it's a great idea to learn a foreign language or to discover any of the things that make our world beautiful and exciting. You might benefit from studies that relate to your job, or maybe you'd rather enjoy a course that takes you to faraway places. And you can earn a degree in night school, too. Even if it's too soon for you to be thinking about college and a career, it's nice to know that there are many different possibilities for you to explore.

A *special note* for girls who would like to learn at the college level but can't afford to attend: You can still learn everything a college student does by asking a local college for a reading list to the courses you're most interested in. You can do all the reading at a library and teach yourself. *College on Your Own* is a helpful book written by Gail Thain Parker and Gene R. Hawks (published by Bantam Books). It tells you how to plan your education at home, how to use college libraries and even study by yourself.

A sense of accomplishment is one of the best ways to start feeling really good about yourself. We get it from looking good, from being knowledgeable, and also from developing a creative talent—a way of expressing ourselves that makes us each a little bit different. I have a friend who has a special talent for painting; another friend of ours is a terrific chef. My favorite hobby is needlepoint. In fact, we each have three inborn talents waiting to be developed. What are yours? If you're not sure of which talent you'd like to express, why not browse through the crafts section of your favorite department store or even look through a book on various crafts? I'm sure you'll find one—or more—that you'd like to try. It can be as traditional and beautiful as embroidery or as exciting and challenging as working in stained glass.

In the chapter on dieting, I mentioned how handy it is to have a hobby to work on every time you want to reach for something to eat. Well, it's really great any time. When I'm feeling blue or bored or depressed or even angry, I work on a needlepoint canvas and find, after a little while, that whatever was bothering me doesn't seem quite as important anymore. The hobby is a way of getting you mind clear so that you can find a soultion more easily.

Did you know that 80 percent of all the people who work or go to school and who don't have a creative interest are unhappy? It's true! We all need something a little bit different that doesn't come under the heading of Work—even if we like our job. It adds a new dimension to our lives, and when we have a finished work of art to enjoy or to share with someone we care about, it fills us with a very special feeling.

Our feelings tell us a lot about the person each of us is— whether we're sensitive and caring, practical and down-to-earth, daring and creative, maybe even all of these. By understanding and accepting yourself, by knowing your limitations, your assets and your weak points, you build your character. Knowing who you are means never compromising your values and your views and being able to explain them to others. It might take a lifetime to find out all about yourself, but that's the fun of living. If we had all the answers now, what would we have to look forward to?

Marie On: Taking Stock of Yourself

Girls who are constantly faced with the question "Who am I?" usually know themselves very well. The problem is that they don't like the girl they see in the mirror. We all tend to exaggerate our faults, but sometimes they can stand in the way of our being our best self. If you often find yourself guilty of being tactless, jealous, insecure, inconsiderate, or even sarcastic and mean, you know that there's a dark side of your character you'd like to keep hidden. But if you don't work to correct it, you'll find it showing at the worst times.

Take stock of yourself. That means drawing up a list of your good points and your bad ones. Concentrate on improving the good and diminishing the bad. Ask yourself why you are catty or sarcastic. Is it a defense against insecurity? Are you insecure about your looks? If so, improve them. Do you find yourself saying the wrong things at the wrong time (tactlessness)? Think before you speak and ask yourself if what you're about to say is appropriate.

It takes practice to move the minuses into the plus column, but it can be done. Just like dieting or studying or improving your voice, you have to practice to be perfect. Not only will it make you feel better about yourself, it will make others more receptive to you.

17.
Our World:
Your Family . . . and Mine

FAMILY, RELIGION, BUSINESS—that's the Osmond order of priorities that has kept my family tightly knit through all our years in show business. Religion plays an important role in my life and in my family's life: It reminds me of who I really am when success tries to go to my head, and it keeps me aware of the need to be close to my family. Religion isn't something you do once a week—it's a way of life, no matter what religion you believe in. Going to church every Sunday doesn't automatically make you a good girl. I live it seven days a week because I'm enthusiastic about it every day. It gives me direction; it feels good to know why I'm here and where I'm going, what life is all about. Religion isn't something that ties me down. Hey—it's fun.

I'm not involved in my church only because it is the church of my parents. I'm not the kind of person who takes someone's word for something—I have to investigate on my own. I went through a period when I wasn't sure, so I studied and found my questions answered. That's why I believe.

Don't misunderstand—I'm not saying that you've got to be a Mormon. I think that believing in God and religion is what's important, whether it's the religion of your family, one you've discovered on your own, or the Church of Jesus Christ of Latter-Day Saints. It gives life meaning and a sense of purpose.

When I meet kids who thank me for showing them the right example and reminding them of their own religion, I know that my work is worthwhile. But when fans tell me that they envy my "glamorous" job, that's when I really start telling them where my priorities are! Show business might seem glamorous on the surface, but there are lots of bruises no one else sees, just as there are for everyone else, no matter what kind of work they

Teaching Bible class with my brother Jay.   PHOTOCRAFT

do. My faith sustains me through these trials as well as through the good times. It's what you have left over after you've removed all the glamor that tells who you really are.

All faiths teach that we must respect our parents. I believe that is the secret to having a close bond with your family. Without these warm ties, you can't really have fulfillment at home— and that's when kids start getting into trouble.

My brothers and I were raised to believe that Mother and Father are equal. Mother devotes her time to us and Father, as head of the household, makes the important decisions. And we respect them both for it. We may not always agree with Father —he may not always be right—but he is always Father, and that gives us a better understanding of each other, all the way round.

I remember one time when Mother wanted me to wear a certain dress, which I thought made me look fat. When I argued about it, Father intervened and said that, no matter how I felt,

189

I should always trust Mother and respect her opinions. "I don't ever want you to disrespect her again," he told me, "It hurts me more than it hurts her." I'll never forget his words because they told me how much he loves and respects my mother and taught me to do the same. Until then, I never realized how much we can hurt our parents, two people who will always know more and have so much to give. Now if I don't agree with my parents' opinion, we sit down and discuss it. I don't think I'll ever be so quick to disregard my parents' wisdom again.

Even though we are all grown, my brothers and myself, my parents try to set the right example for us. They write us letters —whether we're at home or away—and help us make the right decisions, now that we are more responsible. The relationship between you and your parents is never as one-sided as you might think. Sure, at times it seems like your parents give all the orders and kids do all the obeying, but they really love you and only want the best for you. It's often hard to see, but it's worth it, especially when you remember that your parents are doing the best job they can.

Another special time I'll always remember happened not so long ago. I was rehearsing for a television show from 6 A.M. 'til midnight and didn't have time to make my bed for two days— and the clothes were beginning to pile up on a chair in my room. I came home the next evening and found that my parents had changed my sheets and spruced up my room. They had left a note with a flower on my pillow. I realized then that material things—diamond earrings or a new car—aren't the important things in life. The little considerations that we receive from those who love us and whom we love are what counts.

It's hard to get close to your parents if you don't know how to communicate without being hostile, or if you sense hostility in them. It's as though every discussion turns into a confrontation filled with anger that neither you nor your parents really understand. It seems as though only yesterday you were the little child who listened, and all of a sudden, you're rebelling. Because your parents love you, they are all the more confused by your lack of respect and trust; because you feel the need to be grown-up, you want more privacy. There's no one foolproof solution, but there is something I think you'll be interested in: Family Home Evening.

Feelings of closeness can be found again, once you are able to talk to your parents and gain some understanding, on both sides. Even when there is perfect harmony in your home, you don't always have a chance to talk to your brothers, sisters, and parents—everyone is involved in different activities and it's hard sometimes to get together, even at the dinner table. Family Home Evening takes place on Monday evenings and everyone attends! When my brothers all still lived at home, we had one large meeting. Now they have Family Home Evening in their own homes—but we *all* get together once a month! Family Home Evening is always *fun* (we had a luau once), *funny* (because you never know what's going to happen) and *spiritual* in the sense that it's a way of getting closer to your parents and helping them understand you, too. It keeps you thinking in the right perspective.

The Church of Jesus Christ of Latter-Day Saints, the Mormon church, puts out a pamphlet to give you ideas (it's nothing preachy) called, "The Family Home Evening Manual." It's got lots of ideas for parents as well as kids; every family member takes a turn leading the evening's activities. You can write or call the local chapter of this church for the booklet, if you're interested.

Let me tell you about some of the special Family Home Evenings we've had. One night, when we were performing on tour, we had no chance to plan an activity or a discussion. Father was in charge and thought we should all tell each other how we felt. It's sometimes hard to tell your brothers that you love them, especially when it's not something you say all the time, though you feel it constantly. Sometimes we just forget, we take it for granted. We all shared our love for each other that night and couldn't help being overcome by the emotion of the special evening. "I love you" is something that should be said a lot when you really feel it.

An earlier time, Donny and I were "master of ceremonies." We were a lot younger, and it was a special treat to be able to decide the menu for dinner, who would say the opening prayer, where we would each sit (Donny and I were propped on big pillows and everyone else sat on couches). It was fun even though it was a learning experience; we enjoyed having a hint of responsibility.

191

Being an aunt is a great experience, especially when you have nineteen nieces and nephews! PHOTOCRAFT

Last year, when my parents and Jay were on a vacation in the Middle East, Donny, Jimmy, a friend of ours, and I spent Family Home Evening together. We drove our motor home to the lake near our house, roasted marshmallows and hot dogs, and made hot chocolate. We totally ruined the pan we used on the open fire, but we had a great night, talking sincerely about the times we had shared and what the future might bring.

Family Home Evening at my brother Virl's house is what he calls the weekly "interview." It's a time to air any problems that might have come up the week before or just to check that everything is all right. This is how you can apply the idea of Family Home Evening in your home—by gathering with your parents and brothers or sisters to open up the channels of communication. Your "interview" can be a time to discuss all the things that have been bothering you—curfews, privacy, difficulties at school, dating. I think you'll be surprised to find out that your parents have questions, too. Once you are able to talk over problems, you'll see that they aren't as terrible or as one-sided as they seem. And when you and your parents uncover your real feelings for each other, when you hear them say that they really love you even though you don't always get along, you have the beginnings of a very special kind of relationship. Family Home Evening, or your variation of it, is extra important if both your parents work and if your schedule and theirs leaves little time to be together. Setting aside an hour or two each week can give you the closeness of families who see each other more often.

We can create problems with our parents, or we can act in such a way as to prevent them from starting or from growing out of proportion—parents are often set in their ways, leaving it up to us to smooth the way as we mature. I think it's a shame that the antagonism which sometimes exists between us and our parents is harped on by the media, in movies, stories, and television shows, when we should be exploring ways of solving these differences. Maybe emphasizing the "generation gap" makes more interesting news or sells more copies, and maybe that's why the world is in so much trouble today, but we don't have to throw up our arms and accept teen years as being filled with disharmony.

Every family is a little world of its own, and every member has a say in whether or not it's going to be a peaceful one. Maybe none of us has much influence on the outside world, but every one of us is certainly a fair-sized percentage of our own family and can influence that environment to a great extent. Part of loving—and we all love our parents, even if it's temporarily hidden—is caring, and caring and taking care of one another is what life is all about. Someday, most of us will be lucky enough to realize this in terms of romantic love; right now, we can practice it within our family.

The closest bond within our family is the one every girl can have with her mom. When I was unhappy with the way I looked, as I told you about at the beginning of this book, I found out that our mother can be our best friend; she can help us and guide us, if we let her. Even if things have gone wrong in the past, even if your mom works and can't be at home all day, it's never too late or too hard to strengthen your relationship. It's as easy as asking a question in a way that lets Mom know you care about her answer.

When I felt unattractive, my mother was the one who said, "Don't cry, because you can be pretty." Of course, a brother or even a sister will tease because they think that's the way to goad you into doing something positive. It doesn't work! But mothers are more sensitive and helpful. If you're overweight or if your complexion isn't as lovely as it could be, Mom can help by preparing your meals a better way; she can help you consult a professional whether it's a dermatologist (for your skin) or a stylist (to give you a more "with-it" hairstyle); she can quiz you if you're having trouble with your studies, and she can listen to you when your social life looks dim, especially if you ask her what she would do in your situation—Mom likes to know she's still needed, loved, and respected.

It's important to remember that being close doesn't mean talking to Mom as though she were a classmate or girlfriend, or talking to her for as long as you talk to your friends. Sometimes just the way you answer a question or the smile you show as you do a chore reminds you both of how much you care.

My mother is strict and yet loving—a great mom isn't really the one who lets you get away with everything! She has never stopped me from doing what I wanted *if* it was a learning experience—and that's a distinction we kids don't always understand at the time. Mother let me experiment with makeup, though sometimes I wasn't allowed out of the house until it was washed off! She let me learn about fashion by allowing me to pick out my own clothes, but my mistakes usually went back to the store! If Mother saw that I was doing the wrong thing, she would sit down and explain it to me, and I learned to accept her wisdom as I reminded myself that she had been through it all before. It's hard to put your trust in your parents' judgment, especially when you want to wear makeup and start dating and they say no, but it's all part of that sometimes painful, sometimes happy process called "growing up." And when they do give you the okay, you'll appreciate the makeup and the dating, and your parents, even more!

I think it's great that we can always learn something from our mom—she'll always have experienced beforehand things that are new to us. Of course, it can be fun to experience the unknown all by ourselves, but it can also be very difficult. It's the difficult part that parents try to save us from.

Today, I still ask Mother how I can improve myself, and she'll even ask me for my advice. She might be bored to death with my talk of fashion or makeup, but she listens because she knows it interests me, and I listen to her talk about things that are important in her life because I am interested in her. It's this kind of give-and-take that makes a relationship work, with your mother and father, friends, dates, everyone you're likely to meet.

Now, more than ever, I'm able to appreciate much of the advice Mother gave me in the past, whether it was washing my face with a hot towel every night before bed or taking business courses in school. When it seems to you as though you're being told what to do, left and right, remember that your mother will never tell you to do something that's bad for you. You'll understand her concern when you have your own children. I know you've heard that before . . . but it's true! I only hope that I can be as good a mother as mine is—she's pretty hard to top, though.

Sharing is a very personal part of your relationship with your mother. I've found that some of the times when you clamor for privacy are times when you've got something to hide. But if you are honest with yourself, you can be honest with your mother.

When Mother waits up for me to come home from a date, I'm glad. I want to tell her about my evening and she is happy that I've had a good time. She's not resentful that I'm young, because she knows we all are young once. (And I'm sure that life gets better as you get older!) When she asks me if I'd rather she didn't accompany me to a meeting or an appointment, I say of course *not*. I want her with me because I value her guidance every step of the way, and at every age. It's truly a wonderful thing when you know that there's always one special person in your life who'll always be there for you. All it involves is changing your thinking just a little bit to the point where you realize that everything is more fun when you can share with your mom.

Your father can have a very special influence in your life, too. He doesn't always have to say it in so many words because you know he's always there. Sometimes it's difficult to discuss certain things with your father—you might feel more comfortable talking to your mom. But that doesn't mean that you can't have a warm relationship with your father, too. When fathers seem reluctant to let their daughters grow up, it's really because they're afraid of losing them. If you can share the new and exciting happenings in your life with your dad, you'll find that he's more than willing to share his thoughts and advice with you.

I remember important times I have spent with my father, when we would talk about life, about my future, my hopes and dreams. He is there when I'm too tired to talk and when I'm blue—and don't even know why—I just know that I need to hear his reassuring words.

I look to Father for guidance. My friends will tell me that I gave a great performance, but it is Father who will show me how I can improve myself. That's something only he and Mother care enough to say.

There's an old saying that every little girl hopes to marry a man who's just like her father. I know that's true because my father's qualities are the ones I would most cherish in a husband and would try my best to have as a wife.

Brothers and sisters can be an important part of our lives, too. My brothers were, in my mind, an ideal I had to live up to. They never really seemed to notice me (a problem an only sister or a younger one often has), but then, right after I recorded "Paper Roses," I remember my brother Alan complimenting me. I knew I had made my brothers proud—and had made them take notice!

People often ask me the best part of having brothers—well, it's terrific for getting dates! But seriously, it's great to have someone close to you who is going through the same things you are. Family Home Evening can really bring you and your sister or brother closer together—that's a very special relationship you can continue all your lives. Jimmy and I are very close because we're the youngest. We often talk about the things that are important to both of us. He knows that our generation has its share of problems, that too many young people are followers instead of leaders, and that they don't always have the moral guidance they should or a strong sense of direction. Jimmy is young enough not to have been exposed to all the wordly influences yet, but old enough to know what's going on. He has the chance, as we all do, to be one of the new leaders. He has seen the bad things that can happen to kids these days and knows he can make up his own mind.

Younger brothers and sisters are impressionable, but they don't want to be talked down to. I think he appreciates being treated as a young adult. I know that I did, too, and because of it, I felt more willing to listen and understand. I think that if we don't have this willingness, we stop our ability to grow, to be leaders, and to think for ourselves.

I talk very openly with all my brothers. There's nothing we can't say to each other. They are willing to share the things they've learned with me, and they show an interest in the things I've been through. It's a question of learning to appreciate others' points of view. I was a very quiet child because I didn't talk until I really understood what was being said. So I sat in on family and business meetings and I listened. If I was asked to, I spoke, but usually I waited until I could voice a learned opinion. Speaking up and intelligently explaining my opinions was, to me, a sign of growing up. Being part of a family made it that much easier.

Marie On: What Bothers Teens the Most

CHORES

Making my bed in the morning has always been a challenge (translation: nuisance!) to me. But I realized that it's something that has to be done *every* morning and I'd better stop frowning about it. I've learned that we can get the most done when we do any chore right away—putting it off wastes time, and later, when we're running late, we might have to pass up doing something a lot more fun.

Being part of a family means participating in the exciting activities as well as helping out with the boring things like doing the dishes, setting the table, and watching baby sister on an occasional Saturday night. Try to put a smile on your face—it might make the task go a little faster and be a little more pleasant. And remember that doing even a small task well can give you a sense of accomplishment.

ALLOWANCE

It's always hard to keep to a budget, and when you're on an allowance, it's even harder. I've been getting an allowance (clothing and spending money) since I've been dating and going out with friends, so I know what it's like to impose limits on yourself. I often need more than I have, and I have to make a choice when I see two things I want at the same time. When you want to go out with your friends to go shopping, for instance, do what I do when you can't buy—window shop. And if you see something you like, ask the store if they will hold it until you can afford it. Friends will understand—very few girls always get everything they want, even if it seems that way to you.

If family economics are tight, why not get a part-time job after school, like babysitting? You'll have some extra cash and a feeling of independence, too.

I also think it's important to remember that having the latest pair of jeans isn't as vital as we think, even if "all" the other girls have them. But if there is something that you'd really like to have or if basic expenses like bus fare and school supplies take too big a bite out of your allowance, try talking to your parents —that's something we are all able to do.

CURFEWS AND HOME RULES

Parents decide and there's no getting around that for any of us. We can make the best of it, or we can brood about it and not have much fun at all. It's hard to believe that parents know everything when we want to go out on three dates in one week and they say two's the limit, but . . . they are our parents and deserve our respect. I listened to my parents' advice and soon gained enough trust to be allowed to decide for myself what was appropriate. It's hard to accept your parents' decisions at first, when you're afraid of being laughed at by friends with more relaxed rules, but if you're supposed to be in by eleven and your date wants to stay out until eleven-thirty, be prepared to put your foot down. He'll listen if he really wants to be with you. (If it's okay with your parents, why not start the date half an hour earlier?)

SCHOOLWORK

For many years, I had tutors to compensate for not being able to attend regular school. I found that by really concentrating, I was able to get my studies done and out of the way, even while

Setting aside time for "required reading" doesn't have to be a drag. I love the peaceful time I spend in the library, boning up on my favorite subjects.   PHOTOCRAFT

199

learning songs and scripts. In fact, I was so eager to learn that I completed the high school equivalency requirements a year ahead of time. But I also know that school isn't always fun or easy. The secret to making studying more appealing is to approach it with a positive attitude.

Look for the areas within each subject that are the most interesting for you. If you're taking a course in Art History and reading all about it from a boring textbook, go to the library and browse through art books filled with beautiful reproductions. Choose an artist or two whose work you most admire and learn about the history of their times through a biography.

Study with a friend and test each other on material you have to learn for a quiz.

If you're having trouble with your grades, talk to your teachers and explain where you think your weak areas lie. If a teacher understands that you want to do well and are serious, he or she will want to encourage you in the right direction. You might also think about enlisting the aid of an older student—ask your teacher about this, too.

When all else fails, think of schoolwork as a way of making yourself a more intelligent person and a more interesting one— no one likes people who can't talk about anything but themselves!

18.
Our World:
Your Friends Count, Too

THE GIRLS IN your life influence you a lot. You share confidences and experiences, as well as clothes and certain habits (so hopefully, your friends will have only good ones!). My mother is my best friend, but I also spend time with girls my own age.

Luckily, we are all able to choose our friends and we should do so with care. Girls who are attractive attract nice guys; girls with a questionable reputation attract questionable guys. It's just as important to be with the right girls as it is not to be with the wrong ones! You may think I'm exaggerating, but I'm not—guys can tell a lot about a girl (or think they can) by the kind of people she associates with.

I don't believe that you should limit your friendship to just one or two girls. Everyone should have lots of friends—it's more fun that way and you don't feel jealous when a new girl enters the scene. School makes it easy to socialize and discover new people, but if you have trouble making friends in class, join an after-school activity: a sewing club, a dance club, a crafts club. If the activity is a speciality of yours, you can make a new friend by sharing a secret for doing it better. If you're new at it, ask a girl you think you might like for a secret of hers. You can take the direct approach and invite her over to your home after school, for studying or even a snack. Ask a friend of yours to introduce you to a friend of hers; keep the chain going. If you're new in school and want to be part of an interesting group of girls, get involved in one of their activities. When you see them congregate after school, have the courage to walk right over to them and introduce yourself.

Making friends is a lot like going on a diet—once you've done it, you have to consider maintaining it. Of course, friendship is a lot more fun than a diet . . . but they're still similar! Friend-

What better way to get acquainted with new friends—a quilting party!
PHOTOCRAFT

ships are fragile relationships, especially when you're still discovering yourself. Think of how many friends you've had in your life so far . . . and how many of them are your friends today. It's probably not too high a percentage. Why? Because we change, and the circumstances of our lives change. Some of your friends have probably moved away. Others now live in different neighborhoods and attend different schools. You may have lost your first friends over a fight about a book or a toy or a cookie—seems like a long time ago, doesn't it? It's hard to imagine, but some of the friends you have now may not be in your class next year. You may go away to college and find new ones all over again. But while you are enjoying each other's company, you should cherish the relationship, if she's a good friend.

A good friend is not a girl who *expects* you to share your homework answers with her.

A good friend is a girl who offers you her notes when you've lost yours.

A good friend is not a girl who asks you to lie for her when she's in a jam.

A good friend is a girl who supports you when you're feeling down.

A good friend is not a girl who enjoys putting down your other friends and who is possessive of you.

A good friend is a girl who is a lively part of any group and who enjoys meeting new people, as you do.

PHOTOCRAFT

Every relationship is based on give-and-take. It can't be one-sided, or someone feels cheated and that's not what friendship is all about. Friendship concerns loyalty, dependability, and honesty. To have a good friend, you have to be a good friend. But having friends isn't more important than your own self-esteem, and neither is the friendship of girls in a clique.

A clique is a group of girls who set themselves up as the "in" group. That means they amuse themselves by *ex*cluding more girls than they *in*clude. Many girls join cliques to feel that they are part of a group, and they often give up their identity to do it —being in a clique is very definitely being a follower, not a leader. The opinion you have of yourself should mean more than being accepted by a small group of girls who have gotten a certain reputation by being snobby. I was almost pressured into a group like that. I didn't join because I was wanted for my name, not because of the person I am inside. And when I saw the way these girls snubbed all others, I knew that these weren't the kind of friends I wanted. They really aren't friends at all.

Being part of a group can be a lot of fun, if the group is not a clique. Knowing that every Saturday afternoon will be spent ice-skating with your favorite friends is a comfortable pattern, especially at a time when so many things in your life are changing. But what happens when everyone except you decides to try something different, something you don't think is right? When your friends ask you to try drugs or smoke cigarettes or skip a day of school—what do you do?

It may seem like a lonely alternative, but is companionship worth sacrificing your beliefs? It's a question many girls have to answer. Girls who become followers instead of leaders are giving in to the pressure of their fellow classmates. With today's care-free morality, too many kids are tempted in the wrong direction. It can happen very easily: Your friends ask you to join them, you like your friends, so you go along. But what happens to you when you get in trouble? They won't be able to help you any more than they can help themselves. Your good opinion of yourself should mean more to you than your friends' acceptance. Sure, I may be considered the odd one in my group because I don't believe in being promiscuous, but I have my self-respect, and the respect of friends who really count and who share my beliefs.

Did you ever want to be friends with an older girl?

I think there's always one special person in your life who, next to your mother, is a girl you can look up to and learn from. She may be an older sister or cousin, an aunt or even a friend of your parents, as mine was. Her name was Frenda and to me, she was the epitome of everything I wanted to be. When I was ten, she took me to get my nails manicured—I was so impressed and excited that a beautiful woman had taken an interest in a kid like me! She told me that it takes only an extra fifteen minutes to make sure you look your best, to take a bubble bath to smell clean and fresh, to put lotion on your skin, to check your hair and makeup before you leave the house. If you do this, you won't find yourself checking in every mirror all through the day. To show my appreciation, I began to follow Frenda's advice, like taking care to lubricate my nails and cuticles with a vitamin-enriched cream before going to bed.

Frenda got me interested in needlepoint, a craft I love to do even now. And when I learned to make papier-mâché dolls in school, I made one for her as a special "un-birthday" present. I remember seeing her once without any makeup on and still thinking that she was truly a beautiful woman.

There's a fun way to learn about yourself—like the lessons I learned from Frenda. And there's a not-so-fun way, through *criticism*. Girls—young ones, older ones, you and me—are notorious for criticizing others. Some do it softly, others tactlessly. But if you can take criticism with a grain of salt, you can use it to improve yourself.

Are critics ever accurate? Well, other people have the advantage on us in one respect: They can look at us objectively. If you can listen objectively, with an open mind, without getting very defensive, you might be able to see yourself differently. First, don't think of the criticism as a nasty attack that you have to counterattack. Listen thoughtfully to what your friend is saying and try to accept the fact that she is telling you this for your own good. When she's finished, think over what she has said before you reply. If you disagree with her view of the situation, state your point carefully and calmly. If you agree with her, ask her how she would have handled the situation and thank her for her concern. You can return the favor someday. If your critic is malicious in her approach and she's a good friend, think over what she says anyway: There may be some truth in it. But if not, it's better to ignore it. Maybe she's just in a bad mood.

If by now you'd rather sit home and read a good book, don't despair. Your friends have to make the same thoughtful considerations as you do. They'll be certainly willing to meet you halfway!

Marie On: Overcoming Shyness

Shyness is really just another word for fear, the fear of not fitting in, not being accepted or liked. But did you ever stop to think that every girl has probably had the same feelings as you're having right now? No one is totally confident about herself except those who seem to know that they can't let insecurities stand in their way. We have to get over our insecurities even if that means simply ignoring them.

When I felt insecure and afraid of talking to people, I did all I could to make myself look attractive and feel worthwhile—all the things I've told you about in the other sections of this book. When it came time to take the first step forward, I realized that we just have to stand up to that timid little voice inside us, put a smile on our face, and say hello to that girl or group of kids we'd like to meet.

Don't worry about not being "good enough." A true friend is the one who accepts you on your own merits, not because you know all the answers to the history final or have a way with guys or are wearing the "right" clothes. Besides, if you make yourself interesting, by reading and learning, by getting involved with different hobbies and activities, you'll always have something to say and be an asset to every group.

Shyness can seem like snobbishness to girls who don't know you well, but friendliness is never mistaken. A smile still goes a long way, so take a hint from me and show off yours! You'll be surprised at how soon it is returned. Here are some other tips I've learned:

• Build confidence in yourself by doing all you can to develop your personality.

- Don't wait for someone to talk to you. Take the first step, and you won't have to worry about being put on the spot.
- Don't let yourself be held back by the fear of making a mistake. Don't worry about yourself so much—you're great!
- If you're shy because of a personal problem you can't solve yourself, like blemishes that can make any girl self-conscious, ask for help. If you need improvement in a special area—maybe in choosing the right clothes—turn back to the specific section in the book and experiment with my advice.
- Don't fall into the trap of snobbism. Improving your self-confidence by putting others down and building up your own image is really a sign of feelings of inferiority. Try to see the best in others as well as in yourself, and people will return your friendliness.

Marie On: Overcoming Jealousy

We all start turning a little green around the edges every now and then—it's almost expected when your friend gets a new car or a date with Mr. Gorgeous or the lead in the school play. The whole point about jealousy is that it's a normal thing. But it can get out of hand if we let it. The girl who is always jealous of others because she constantly puts herself down is heading for a lot of disappointment that she can avoid on her own. Think of all the things you have that your friend might not—a special talent, a better relationship with parents, a pretty smile. If you're envious of a friend's shiny hair, do something to improve your own style. You might even ask the envied friend for her beauty secrets; I think you'll find that she goes to a lot of trouble to make her hair look so nice. What you see on the surface is only a very small part of the true story waiting to be told. If you try to remember that, the next time you find yourself thinking All my friends can stay out past midnight—have a car—their own phone—a bigger allowance, you'll realize that maybe they're missing out on something more important that you have.

Here are some sayings I try to remind myself of when I begin to turn green.

- When you are jealous of something a friend has, ask yourself if you would really want it and use it or just wish you were the one showing off.
- If you feel sorry for yourself, you won't be able to think of ways to reach the goals you envy others for.
- You're really not the only girl in your class without a date, for instance, even if you think you are. Do everything *you* can to make yourself interesting (this doesn't include envying the most popular girls in class), and you won't have to worry any more.
- Accept that you are who you are and that you can't become the girl next door. Make friends with yourself—that's the only way to begin making friends with others.

19.
Our World: Waiting for Dating

To ME, DATING is something you have to get out of your system. By the time you get married, you should be completely sure that you have found the right person—someone who makes you happier than ever before, who has a great personality and who understands you perfectly, someone with whom you have so much in common that you'll never want to look at another guy again. Well, I'm going to look the world over before I even think about getting married, and the easiest way to do that is by dating a lot.

Because I know there's a someone out there for me, I'm not worried about getting dates. If a date doesn't get along well with me, I'm still glad we saw each other because it helps me to know what to look for in a guy, in the future. That's why we date: to learn what we like and don't like in a guy, and also to learn about ourselves. I keep a journal so I can look back and see just what discoveries I have made. I double-date a lot with my brothers and they're helpful afterward; they tell me if I neglected my date, if I monopolized the conversation . . . That's the importance of dating.

Dating

Waiting for dating. I don't believe in dating until you're sixteen, and then only double-dates, until you're eighteen. You really don't know how to handle yourself until then. Sure I did some socializing before that: ice-skating with a group, going to a party or a dance; these are another part of the social scene. Dating has to be approached slowly and carefully or else it could go to your head.

The fun of double-dating. My first dates were double-dates. Single-dating is fun and important when you're old enough and when you want to see how well you react with a certain guy. But I still double-date, especially if I don't know my date well but want to. (In case he turns out to be a drip, you can still have a good time if you like the other couple.)

When you first begin to date, you're experiencing something new and different that you want to know more about but can only learn from experience. In a group, you can feel more comfortable, particularly when you're not sure of what to say or how to react. If the conversation between you and your date lags, it's not as noticeable as it would be if you two were alone. The other couple can make up for it, and you can participate in their conversation. And if you see that the other couple is in distress, you can help them out. When I'm with a girl who seems intimidated, I try to involve her in my conversation.

To distinguish *yourself* in a group of four or more, first be sure that you're with people you like (at least the other girl or guy). A lot of laughing and having a good time—that's what dating should be about.

Then, find an interesting topic to talk about. Don't be afraid to speak—no one's going to judge you on the basis of one statement, but that statement will get you into a conversation. With a little foresight, you can find out what interests your date and do a little research on the subject. If he likes basketball, watch a game and pick up on the basics. If he's interested in politics, watch a morning interview program and keep up with newspaper items on world affairs. And remember, your own interests are important and worth talking about too. You may just find that your love for music or soccer or gourmet cooking is something your new date also shares.

But how do you attract guys in the first place? You're probably thinking. I've asked my brothers this question many times. My brothers aren't male chauvinists (I wouldn't let them be!), but they do want their dates to look feminine. Straggly hair, a sloppy T-shirt, and a pair of faded jeans is a real turn-off. So if you want to attract a gorgeous guy, start by making yourself gorgeous!

It is a girl's responsibility to look her best, as it's her decision to say "yes" or "no" when she's asked on a date. It might be a guy's decision to ask us, but we have the final choice! They say it's a man's world . . . but we girls control it too.

But remember that developing your outer beauty isn't everything. I know a girl who is so beautiful, it's hard not to feel plain in comparison. But she has no personality. She has relied totally on her physical attributes, so that talking with her is boring. Every guy wants to date her once, just to be seen with that pretty a girl, but they're not interested after that one time. They get tired of watching her look at herself in every mirror they pass!

You don't have to be ravishing to get dates. I've seen lots of average-looking girls on the arms of very attractive guys. And I know why: because these girls have all made the most of their personality. They're beautiful on the inside and guys know that's more important than physical beauty, that it will last after a pretty girl's looks are gone.

How to meet guys. I know that not every girl is lucky enough to have seven older brothers! If you're an only child, or the oldest, you have to put forth a little effort. Here are some everyday places to consider:
• the library
• church outings
• school dances
• college campus
• sports clubs

Expand your personality so you'll feel comfortable in every kind of situation. Take a class in history or politics: you'll learn something interesting and meet new people at the same time. Did you ever think of joining a hiking club or maybe explore camping? You don't have to look like a sophisticated beauty all the time; it's okay to look casual and sporty as long as your clothes are neat.

When you see a guy you'd like to meet. Smile. Say hello. Ask a friend to introduce you. I don't like taking more of a first move than that, or acting pushy. If you smile at a guy, he'll respond. If he doesn't or if he tries to "play it cool," he's not worth your time. You can let him know you're interested in a polite way by commenting on a class assignment, a favored teacher, a book he is reading. *Don't* go up to a guy and say, "Hi, gorgeous, want to go out with me?" That's not subtle. You can have confidence in yourself without acting brash. *Don't* be intimidated—guys are far from perfect.

In other words, be yourself.

The games you shouldn't play. Playing games might have been

211

okay in grade school, but when guys and girls start to play games with each other, as they start to mature and date, they find that playing with human emotions isn't fun.

I admit that I've been at fault in this respect. I used to play a little game. It went like this: I'll wonder why a certain guy hasn't called recently, and I'll decide that when he does, I won't be home to him.

Now who knows why he hasn't been able to call? Maybe his studies have been keeping him busy. So who's losing out then? Me! That's why you should get out of the playing-games habit, if it sounds familiar to you.

I often have the problem of letting a guy know that I don't put on airs, that I don't go around saying things like, "I'm Marie Osmond. I have to be taken to the best restaurants!" I think that attitude is the worst. I'm just as happy taking a walk on the beach or having burgers after a movie. If you're a popular girl, well known at school, make sure guys don't just naturally assume you're out of reach.

When you have to say "no." If you have an honest excuse, like a previous engagement, be courteous. Say something like, "I'm sorry but I'm busy. I'd like to do it another time soon." *Don't* flaunt your other date—he'll take it as a rejection and say to himself, I don't need this kind of hurt; I sure won't ask her out again. If you're sweet about it, he'll know that you're a popular girl whom guys like to date and that you're still interested in him.

Don't ever feel guilty about turning down a date with a guy you really don't like. Just remember to do it carefully because you don't want to hurt his feelings. One of my brothers' friends asked a girl out and was answered with, "No, thanks. I have a better date for that evening." He told my brothers and his other friends about how cruel she was when she turned him down— put him down was more like it. So not only did she hurt his feelings, she damaged her own reputation as well.

If you find out that a certain guy isn't right for you in the middle of a date, you have to be even more tactful. I once had lunch with a guy who spent the whole time asking me questions I couldn't possibly have known how to answer, such as legal matters. In between questions, he would tell me how dumb I was! When I tried to lighten the lunch with a few funny lines, he said that I cracked too many jokes! "Well, hello Mr. Stuffy,"

I felt like saying. I also felt like leaving after fifteen minutes! He was the type of insecure guy who inflates his ego by putting down those around him. (Even some handsome guys do this—I guess it's what keeps them believing they're wonderful! Or maybe underneath that gorgeousness, they don't feel confident at all.) But I knew that I couldn't be mean; I wouldn't be there to defend myself when he decided to get even by telling his side of the story to his friends. So I sat through the lunch and politely asked to be taken home afterward. That afternoon reinforced my faith in double-dating when you don't know the guy well enough!

Remember, guys talk. And you want them to be able to say only nice things about you.

GOING STEADY

Going steady . . . is for the birds! At least until you're seriously thinking of marriage. Until then, you need time to date lots of guys, to discover the qualities you want in a husband, and which qualities in other people bring out the best ones in you. You have to be a good judge before you commit yourself to one person; you have to be able to see compatibility between you and your special friend. While you're young, you might think that you know yourself well and know what you want, but chances are that your feelings, your emotions, your personality are all still changing and maturing. A guy you thought you were crazy about at seventeen might turn you off at nineteen, after you've been to college or have traveled. Can you think of anything worse than finding this out too late?

Too often, going steady means security; you'll always be sure of a date for the dance. But this shows an *in*security in you. We all get insecure at times—it happens to me when I meet people. (I worry that they're not trying to get to know *me*, only Marie Osmond the celebrity, or that they'll be too critical of me.) But insecurities can't be solved by going steady. The really insecure girl will constantly wonder if he really likes her or not! You have to work at developing your personality, making it stronger 'cause if you don't, you'll never be happy with your boyfriends or with yourself.

213

Playing the field—the football field, that is!   PHOTOCRAFT

SELF-RESPECT

Going steady puts a girl in an awkward position. It makes her too available. I once knew a girl with a very low opinion of herself. The truth was that she could have been very attractive, but she didn't want to bother. She would rather eat than do something with her looks. She didn't enjoy schoolwork, so she didn't improve her mind either. What she did do was run into the first relationship that presented itself, and she got into trouble.

I know other girls who throw themselves at guys, and it's so unattractive. It says: Sex is all I'm worth. It shows a lack of self-respect, and you can be sure that without that, guys won't have

214

any respect for you either. If I'm not attractive enough for him as I am without sex, you should say to yourself, too bad for him! You'll find someone else. A guy who thinks he's worth your sacrificing your opinion of yourself . . . isn't worth it.

The old saying is true: Guys respect good girls. So if you want a good guy, you have to be a good girl! Respect your curfew. Tell him what it is and be sure that he'll respect it, too. If I tell a date that I have to be in at eleven-thirty and he thinks I'm joking, I explain to him that I'm not! That's the way it is—besides, there's nothing you can do after eleven-thirty that you can't do before! It shouldn't be any more fun to be with him at a later hour. When girls tell me that they'd like to be able to stay out until three in the morning, I say that's ridiculous.

Girls should make themselves more desirable; loose behavior doesn't do that. Today, girls are too available, too easy. You should think more highly of yourself.

LOVE AND MARRIAGE

When you're young, it's easy to confuse love with desire. It's not necessary to rush into kissing. I would certainly never make a guy feel that he had to kiss me goodnight.

I once was dating a guy for about a month, once a week. Each date would be less fun as our differences of opinion seemed greater. We finally realized we had nothing in common and couldn't believe it had taken us so long to realize it. What would have happened if there had been any physical involvement? It would have masked our differences until it was too late. That's why I say that limiting yourself to one guy before you're really sure is wrong.

What is real love? I learned about it from my parents. It means being best friends as well as lovers. Being able to give of yourself freely and know that the other person feels the same way. Being able to talk about anything or being able to sit in the same room without feeling the need to talk. Never wanting to stop sharing and giving to each other. A love that lasts forever.

And when I say forever, I mean forever. Too many people are trivializing marriage. They say that marital relationships have a beginning and an end—I say baloney! A relationship dies only if you let it. Love lasts for eternity, not five or six years! If it ends too soon, it was probably because you never really loved each other—maybe the attraction was only physical (the worst reason in the world to get married).

Why do some people get married too soon? Because they go steady for a little while, and as physical desires get stronger, they are faced with a choice of getting married or getting in trouble. Or because, after going steady too early on, they find that marriage is the thing to do (boredom is the second worst reason to get married).

Why not have sex without marriage? Because, if you believe in God and the Ten Commandments, you can't put new words on old sins. What was true yesterday is the same today and tomorrow. I don't know who invented the "new morality" but I know it's not for me. And sex is still only a fraction of what love is all about.

When you find your real love, the one that's going to last, you'll feel it, and you'll also be able to recognize it mentally, thanks to all the experience and knowledge dating has given you.

Marie On: The Manners of Dating

It's fun and exciting to talk about dating, but there's a practical side to it that's not as interesting, but very necessary. Etiquette. That means knowing how to act on every occasion, in all different situations.

Here are some ways you can really impress your date—whether you're out with a guy or your parents or a friend.

POLITENESS

A polite manner will go further toward impressing people than the most fashionable outfit or the fanciest makeup. Being polite often means overlooking the actions of others, if they are inappropriate. Don't call attention to someone's mistake; don't point out your friend's faults publicly. It also means speaking clearly, in a pleasant tone of voice. Language is important. Girls who swear show a lack of intelligence. It says to those you're with, "I don't know enough to use more constructive words." If you speak with precision, color, and confidence, you won't need to use coarse language.

Be polite when you are introduced to someone, even if you don't think you will like the person. It's a matter of courtesy that shows you have grace. It's easy to pick a person apart, but the girl who finds something nice to say about everyone shows character in herself.

Being polite means seeing to it that the people you are with are comfortable. Learn how to introduce one friend to another. (The older or more respected person is told the name of the other first: "Aunt Billie, this is my friend Cathy. Cathy, my aunt, Billie Miller.") When you are introduced to someone, smile, extend your hand, and look at the person's eyes to indicate your attention.

For every occasion, remember these important, yet easily forgotten words: Please, Thank you, and You're welcome.

POISE

Being comfortable and at ease with yourself gives you the feeling of poise. You're in control. When you know that you look your best, you carry yourself with self-confidence, or poise. Your shoulders are straight (not slouched), your gestures are natural, and your stride is sure. People will notice you when you walk into a room, if you have this characteristic.

Poise is also letting others have confidence and do what is right. Let your date help you on with your coat. Be gracious, not clumsy, when he offers to open your car door. (How to get into a car: With your back to the seat, lower yourself onto it and then swing your legs inside.) When you walk into a restaurant, (or anywhere with a door), let your date open it for you (unless, of course, he's carrying a million packages and your arms are free!). It shows courtesy on his part, and most young guys like to display a little chivalry. Girls can accept courtesies and still feel capable and free.

Learn which utensils in a restaurant are for what course. The easiest way to remember is to use the outside silverware first, working your way toward utensils directly next to the plate. To help you further, remember that the long, thin forks are for the main dish; the shorter, wider ones are for salad or your appetizer. The small, blunt-edged knife is for butter; the long sharp

217

one is for cutting. The smallest spoon is for stirring beverages; the larger oval one is for eating puddings or compotes; the large rounded one is for soup.

When you goof: Have a sense of humor about it. Be able to admit your mistake and say, "Wasn't that silly of me." Then forget it—it really isn't important. There's nothing funny or gracious about spending the rest of the evening apologizing for something your date will probably have forgotten a minute later. That ability to laugh at yourself is part of having poise, too. It's not always easy. During the course of one dinner, I managed to drop food on my date's chair twice! It was after a very long day of rehearsals and I was tired, but . . . twice! Yet I was still able to have a positive attitude and not bawl myself out for it the rest of the evening.

Be the best you can, accept yourself, and everyone else will, too.

20.

Memo from Marie:
A Success the Way You Are

KNOW YOURSELF. Be yourself. Enjoy yourself. That way, you'll always put your best image forward. But don't ever limit yourself. There's so much to learn—that's the most important lesson of all.

Change is inevitable. We change as we go from our teens into

PHOTOCRAFT

our twenties, and every year afterward. Our experiences make the most significant changes in our personalities; they have to be lived by each of us. I can tell you about the ones that have influenced me, but you'll have to find out a lot of things for yourself. Our parents try to teach and counsel us, and that's good. Their advice can make it easier for us. But life keeps coming up with new challenges that no one could ever have dreamed of. You can only be prepared for them. Your answers and your decisions will count, too. Once you're confident about yourself, as I hope you are after reading this book, you'll be able to meet those challenges. You may not always be right, but you will always learn from them. Even though you're just starting out, the values and beliefs you discover now will stay with you for all time—they add up to a wisdom that you will be able to share with your children later on.

I've tried to tell you how I've felt, growing up in this complicated world, and what I've learned. The secret to becoming the kind of girl everyone likes to be with (especially you!) is being true to yourself, finding out who you are, not covering yourself over with the image of the person you think you'd like to be. A girl who is sincere and sensitive, who is honest and has integrity, who likes herself and likes people is a difficult person to be. Anyone can be mean and disagreeable, seeing only the bad and taking advantage of others' weaknesses. To be what I call a "good girl" involves a lot of work: It means thinking of others as well as yourself, taking the time to consider your character and work on it, if you find it lacking in the better qualities. It means putting forth the effort to develop yourself and not being content with the fuzzy picture you see in the mirror.

Life is a lot of fun, if you know how to enjoy it. Feeling pretty and looking pretty is the best possible start. You're able to share these good feelings with those around you—your family and your friends. And those are the people who make your life happy. With a positive attitude, you feel as though there's nothing you can't accomplish, if you really want to. It's a special kind of high that only you can give yourself—it doesn't come from anything artificial, but from within. Most of us aren't fortunate enough to feel it all the time—if we did, we could not tell the difference between feeling happy and feeling blue. But we can experience it often. I get it from helping someone less privileged, by knowing that I've done my best at a special task, by taking care to look my best and by making someone happy with a smile. You can, too.

Marie's Maxims

- Know yourself—your likes and your dislikes. And stick to them. Don't change yourself to gain the approval of friends or a date; your opinions are more important.

- Learn to get along with others. Your family and your friends can help you be the girl you most want to be.

- From makeup to manners, practice makes it *all* perfect. Keep at it until you excel.

- Finding good qualities in others is what shows character in you.

- Life keeps getting better as you pass each hurdle and lift yourself from every pitfall.

- Game playing is for the insecure. Be as honest with those you meet as you are with yourself.

- Life has to be balanced, like the four legs of a chair . . . or else. Keep the mental, physical, spiritual, and social you each on an equal par. Some girls care only about dates and neglect their schoolwork—that makes high school a waste. And if all I cared about was my career, I would be a boring person! I keep the private Marie's head level by doing other interesting things: sewing, designing, school courses. Every aspect of my personality, and yours, has to be developed to make us well-rounded individuals.

- Reaching for a new measure of success means being able to change, to improve. Never lose sight of a faraway goal that you want to reach. Keep striving for it by stopping yourself every once in a while and asking the question, How have I bettered myself in the last month? And then, What can I do next!

- Challenge, the adventure of something new, is the most exciting kind of hope. It extends to us a promise, a dream for something better, more wonderful than the last. For me, this past year, it was making a film, *A Gift of Love*, a chance to develop my talents as an actress. In the future is the challenge of marriage, of having a family, of finishing my education, and perhaps adding a new dimension to my career as a performer.

What does the future hold for you? That's your decision . . . because every possibility is within your grasp. All you have to do is reach!